SCHOLASTIC
LITERACY SKILLS

Comprehension
Year 1–2

G000253784

TERMS AND CONDITIONS

IMPORTANT – PERMITTED USE AND WARNINGS – READ CAREFULLY BEFORE USING

Minimum system requirements:

- PC or Mac with CD-ROM drive (16x speed recommended) and 512MB RAM
- P4 or G4 processor
- Windows 2000/XP/Vista or Mac OSX 10.3 or later

For all technical support queries, please phone Scholastic Customer Services on 0845 6039091.

Author
Donna Thomson

Texts chosen by
Elspeth Graham

Editor
Rachel Mackinnon

Assistant editors
Vicky Butt and Louise Titley

CD-ROM design and development team
Joy Monkhouse, Anna Oliwa,
Micky Pledge, Rebecca Male, Allison Parry,
Shoo Fly Publishing and Haremi

Series designers
Shelley Best and Anna Oliwa

Book design team
Shelley Best, Andrea Lewis and Sonja Bagley

Illustrations
Cathy Hughes/Beehive Illustration

Designed using Adobe Indesign
Published by Scholastic Ltd, Villiers House,
Clarendon Avenue, Leamington Spa,
Warwickshire CV32 5PR
www.scholastic.co.uk

Printed by Bell & Bain Ltd, Glasgow
Text © 2009 Donna Thomson
© 2009 Scholastic Ltd
2 3 4 5 6 7 8 9 0   9 0 1 2 3 4 5 6 7 8

British Library Cataloguing-in-Publication Data
A catalogue record for this book is available from
the British Library.
ISBN 978-1407-10050-0

Mixed Sources
Product group from well-managed
forests and other controlled sources
www.fsc.org   Cert no. TT-COC-002769
© 1996 Forest Stewardship Council

Acknowledgements

The publishers gratefully acknowledge permission to reproduce the following
copyright material: **Andersen Press** for the use of text and illustration from
Dr Xargle's Book of Earthlets by Jeanne Willis © text 1988, Jeanne Willis ©
illustration 1988, Tony Ross (1988, Andersen Press). **HarperCollins Publishers**
for the use of text and illustrations from *The Weather Forecast* by Elspeth
Graham and Mal Peet, text © 1996, Elspeth Graham, illustrations © 1996, Mal
Peet (1996, Collins Educational) and text and illustrations from *I'm sorry* by
Sam McBratney and Jennifer Eachus, text © 2000, Sam McBratney, illustrations
© 2000, Jennifer Eachus (2000, HarperCollins). **Hodder and Stoughton
Ltd** for the use of illustrations from *Blue Balloon* by Mick Inkpen © 1989,
Mick Inkpen (1989, Hodder & Stoughton). **Macmillan Children's Books** for
the use of an extract and illustrations from *The Gruffalo* by Julia Donaldson
& Axel Scheffler, text © 1999, Julia Donaldson, illustrations © 1999, Axel
Scheffler (1999, Macmillan Children's Books). **Penguin Group UK** for the use
of illustrations and text from *Father Christmas* by Raymond Briggs © 1973,
Raymond Briggs (1973, Hamilton; 2003, Puffin); an illustration from *Cops and
Robbers* by Janet and Allan Ahlberg, illustration © 1977, Janet Ahlberg (1999,
Puffin) and an extract and illustrations from *Burglar Bill* by Janet and Allan
Ahlberg © text and illustrations 1977, Janet and Allan Ahlberg (1999, Puffin
Books). **Random House Group** for the use of a text extract and illustrations
from *Traction Man is Here* by Mini Grey © 2005, Mini Grey (2005, Jonathan
Cape) and text and illustrations from *Where the wild things are* by Maurice
Sendak © 1967, Maurice Sendak (1967, Bodley Head). **Rockpool Children's
Books** for the use of text and illustration from *My perfect pet* by Stuart Trotter
© 2006, Stuart Trotter (2006, Rockpool Children's Books). **Pamela Todd
Agency** for the use of an illustration by Jill Murphy from *Peace at Last* by Jill
Murphy © 1980, 1995, 2007, Jill Murphy (1980, Macmillan Children's Books).
Walker Books for the use of text and illustrations from *Smelly Jelly Smelly Fish*
by Michael Rosen and Quentin Blake, text © 1986, Michael Rosen, illustrations
© 1986, Quentin Blake (1986, Walker Books); text and illustrations from
The Drive, *Eating Out* and *Playschool*, all by Helen Oxenbury © 1983, Helen
Oxenbury (1983, Walker Books); the cover of *Has anyone here seen William?*
by Bob Graham © 1988, Bob Graham (1998, Walker Books) and for the use
of the cover illustration from *Has anyone here seen William?* by Bob Graham
© 1988, Blackbird Design Pty Ltd (1988, Walker Books). Every effort has been
made to trace copyright holders for the works reproduced in this book, and
the publishers apologise for any inadvertent omissions.

Contents

INTRODUCTION.. 4

FRAMEWORK OBJECTIVES 6

Chapter 1
Retelling

INTRODUCTION 8

WHO, WHAT, WHERE?..............................10

PROBLEM AND RESOLUTION.....................14

RETELLING INSTRUCTIONS........................18

SEQUENCING 22

Chapter 2
Literal questioning

INTRODUCTION 26

'WHO' QUESTIONS 28

'WHAT' QUESTIONS 32

'WHERE' QUESTIONS 36

'WHO', 'WHAT' AND 'WHERE' QUESTIONS 40

Chapter 3
Prediction

INTRODUCTION 44

WHAT HAPPENS NEXT? 46

RHYTHM AND RHYME 50

CLUES FROM THE COVER 54

READING SIGNS AND SYMBOLS..................58

Chapter 4
Inference

INTRODUCTION 62

SEEKING MEANING 64

FINDING CLUES 68

PRESENTING EVIDENCE............................ 72

HOW I KNOW 76

Chapter 5
Clarification

INTRODUCTION...80

MAKING SENSE..82

SIMILAR MEANING 86

SKIMMING AND SCANNING.......................90

SKIMMING AND SCANNING FOR

SIMILAR MEANINGS 94

Chapter 6
Evaluation

INTRODUCTION 98

CHARACTERS' FEELINGS 100

WHAT YOU THINK................................. 104

CHARACTERS' THOUGHTS....................... 108

EVALUATION QUESTIONS............................. 112

Chapter 7
Review

INTRODUCTION 116

FICTION AND NON-FICTION......118

NURSERY RHYMES

AND STORIES.....................123

Introduction

The Scholastic Literacy Skills: Comprehension series

Comprehension is the ability to understand and elicit meaning from any type of written or illustrated material. It is the reason for reading. If readers can read the words but do not understand what they mean, they are not really reading.

This series offers teachers carefully structured guidance on how to use the essential comprehension skills of summarising, predicting, clarifying and questioning to extract the author's meaning. Each book is progressive and supports the teaching and development of these comprehension strategies. The series also offers teachers a generic framework for teaching reciprocal reading – a process that provides children with the confidence to explore and enjoy a range of 'real' books beyond the samples featured in the series. The skills pages show the children how to gather information, respond to questions meaningfully and generate their own literal, inferential and evaluative questions from quality fiction and non-fiction extracts. It also provides levelled comprehension assessment materials that correlate with NC reading age levels.

Overview of the teaching of comprehension

To fully engage children in the reading process and help them to explore and make sense of a range of text, they need to understand the skills involved in how we make meaning. Alongside summarising, clarifying and predicting, they need to be able to identify and apply the three fundamental questioning skills:

- Literal – explicit meaning. (Who? What? Where?)
- Inference – hidden and implied meaning. (Detective work – thinking and searching for clues to make deductions. Why? How do you know that?)
- Evaluation – personal meaning. (Using own experience to explain events or characters' actions, feelings and behaviour and linking them to the author's viewpoint. Why do you think…?)

These skills enable children to have full understanding of information, whether it is presented through text or pictures and are central to bringing meaning and reasoning to learning to read and learning in general.

Comprehension is not something that happens after reading. Good readers use their experience and knowledge of the world, alongside their knowledge of vocabulary and language structure, to make sense of the text and relate to the author's viewpoint. Good readers monitor their understanding as they read and know how to resolve their difficulties with comprehension as the problems arise.

About the product

This book contains seven chapters. Each chapter focuses on a different aspect of comprehension, and is organised into four sections with clear objectives, background information, teaching ideas and photocopiable pages for use in whole-class teaching, with groups or for independent work. Each chapter also features a poster.

Posters

Each chapter has one poster which relates to the subject of the chapter. It should be displayed and used for reference throughout the work on the chapter. The poster notes (on the chapter opening page) offer suggestions for how they could be used. There is a black and white version in the book and full-colour version on the CD-ROM for you to print or display on a whiteboard.

Activities

Each section contains two activities. These activities all take the form of a photocopiable page which is in the book and on the CD-ROM for you to display or print out (these pages are also provides with answers where appropriate). Over thirty of the photocopiable pages have linked interactive activities on the CD-ROM. These interactive activities are designed to act as starter activities to the lesson, giving whole-class support on the information being taught. However, they can also work equally well as plenary activities, reviewing the work the children have just completed.

Using the CD-ROM

Below are brief guidance notes for using the CD-ROM. For more detailed information, see **How to use** on the start-up screen, or **Help** on the relevant screen for information about that page.

The CD-ROM follows the structure of the book and contains:

- All of the photocopiable pages, with answers where appropriate.
- All of the poster pages in full colour.
- Over thirty interactive on-screen activities linked to the photocopiable pages.

Getting started

To begin using the CD-ROM, simply place it in your CD- or DVD-ROM drive. Although the CD-ROM should auto-run, if it fails to do so, navigate to the drive and double-click on the red **Start** icon.

Start-up screen

This is the first screen where you can access: terms and conditions, registration link, how to use the CD-ROM and credits. If you agree to the terms and conditions, click **Start** to continue.

Main menu

Clicking on the relevant **Chapter** icon will take you to the chapter screen where you can access the posters and the chapter's sections. Clicking on **All resources** will take you to a list of all the resources, where you can search by key word or a specific resource.

Section screen

Upon choosing a section from the chapter screen, you are taken to a list of resources for that section. Here you can access all of the photocopiable pages and interactive activities linked to that section.

Resource finder

This lists all of the resources on the CD-ROM. You can:

- Select a chapter and/or section by selecting the appropriate title from the drop-down menus.
- Search for key words.
- Scroll through the list of resources.
- Launch a resource by clicking once on its row.

Navigation

The resources (poster pages, photocopiable pages and interactive activities) all open in separate windows on top of the menu screen. To close a resource, click on the **x** in the top right-hand corner. To return to the menu screen you can either close or minimise a resource.

Closing a resource will not close the program. However, if you are in a menu screen, then clicking on the **x** will close the program. To return to a previous menu screen, you need to click on the **Back** button.

Whiteboard tools

The CD-ROM comes with its own set of whiteboard tools for use on any whiteboard.
These include:

- Pen tool
- Highlighter tool
- Eraser
- Sticky note

Click on the **Tools** button at the foot of the screen to access these tools.

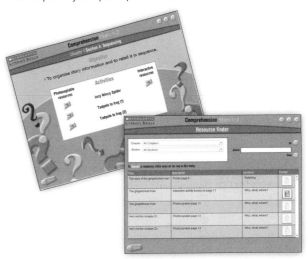

Printing

Print the resources by clicking on the **Print** button. The photocopiable pages print as A4 portrait pages, but please note that a landscape poster or photocopiable page needs the orientation set to landscape in your print preferences. The interactive activities will print what is on the screen. For a full A4 printout you need to set the orientation to landscape in your print preferences.

Framework objectives

Page	Section	Literacy skills objective	Strand 7 (Y1): Identify the main events and characters in stories, and find specific information in simple texts.	Strand 7 (Y1): Use syntax and context when reading for meaning.	Strand 7 (Y1): Make predictions showing an understanding of ideas, events and characters.	Strand 8 (Y1): Visualise and comment on events, characters and ideas, making imaginative links to their own experiences.	Strand 7 (Y2): Draw together ideas and information from across a whole text, using simple signposts in the text.	Strand 7 (Y2): Give some reasons why things happen or characters change.	Strand 8 (Y2): Explain their reactions to texts, commenting on important aspects.
10	Who, what, where?	To retell using key questions to highlight the main points of a story: Who? What? Where?	✓						
14	Problem and resolution	To retell, extending the main 'who', 'what' and 'where' points of a story to include theme, conflict and resolution.	✓				✓		
18	Retelling instructions	To organise non-fiction information and to retell it in the correct order.	✓						
22	Sequencing	To organise story information and to retell it in sequence.	✓				✓		
28	'Who' questions	To identify literal information about characters within pictures. To gather, organise and classify this information to respond to and formulate questions.	✓				✓		
32	'What' questions	To identify literal information about what the characters are doing within pictures. To gather, organise and classify this information in order to respond to questions and formulate own questions.	✓				✓		
36	'Where' questions	To identify literal information about where the characters are within pictures. To gather, organise and classify this information in order to respond to and formulate questions.	✓				✓		
40	'Who', 'what' and 'where' questions	To identify literal key word information about characters, action and place within text. To gather, organise and classify this information in order to respond to and formulate questions.	✓				✓		
46	What happens next?	To find clues from images that suggest what might happen next.			✓				
50	Rhythm and rhyme	To look for clues in text and pictures that suggest what might happen next.			✓				
54	Clues from the cover	To show how to look for clues in pictures and the title of a book to predict what to expect from the story or information inside.			✓				
58	Reading signs and symbols	To predict warning, information and instruction from picture symbols and signs.			✓				

Chapter 1 (pages 10–22) · **Chapter 2** (pages 28–40) · **Chapter 3** (pages 46–58)

Framework objectives

Chapter	Page	Section	Literacy skills objective	Strand 7 (Y1): Identify the main events and characters in stories, and find specific information in simple texts.	Strand 7 (Y1): Use syntax and context when reading for meaning.	Strand 7 (Y1): Make predictions showing an understanding of ideas, events and characters.	Strand 8 (Y1): Visualise and comment on events, characters and ideas, making imaginative links to their own experiences.	Strand 7 (Y2): Draw together ideas and information from across a whole text, using simple signposts in the text.	Strand 7 (Y2): Give some reasons why things happen or characters change.	Strand 8 (Y2): Explain their reactions to texts, commenting on important aspects.
Chapter 4	64	Seeking meaning	To identify and interpret inferred meaning from picture clues to better understand the author's intention.				✓	✓	✓	
Chapter 4	68	Finding clues	To identify and interpret inferred meaning from text clues and pictures in order to respond to questions.				✓	✓	✓	
Chapter 4	72	Presenting evidence	To gather and present evidence that (a) justifies answers given to inference questions and (b) indicates a full understanding of the author's intention.			✓		✓		
Chapter 4	76	How I know	To gather, organise and classify inferred information in order to formulate questions and answers from text.			✓	✓	✓	✓	
Chapter 5	82	Making sense	To make sense of unfamiliar words and images using contextual clues.		✓					
Chapter 5	86	Similar meanings	To make sense of contextual clues that have similar meanings.		✓					
Chapter 5	90	Skimming and scanning	To answer literal questions from text by skimming and scanning to locate the same words as the key words that appear in the question.					✓		
Chapter 5	94	Skimming and scanning for similar meanings	To learn how to skim and scan information to locate key words and clues. To link clues that have similar meanings to support deduction. To infer from clues to answer questions.					✓		
Chapter 6	100	Characters' feelings	To draw on own experience to interpret characters' emotions and actions within picture narrative in order to explain what is happening or may happen next.				✓	✓		✓
Chapter 6	104	What you think	To understand that an evaluation question asks for the use of literal and inference skills, and personal experience to think about a character's feelings or actions.				✓	✓		✓
Chapter 6	108	Characters' thoughts	To identify characters' motives from words and images in order to support understanding of evaluation within text and pictures.				✓	✓	✓	✓
Chapter 6	112	Evaluation questions	To understand that evaluation questions mean thinking about characters' feelings or actions by using literal and inference skills and personal experiences to ask and answer questions from text and pictures.				✓	✓	✓	✓
Chapter 7	118	Fiction and non-fiction	To identify the plot and sequence of events within picture stories. To gather clues and information from non-fiction pictures and text to answer questions.	✓		✓	✓	✓	✓	✓
Chapter 7	123	Nursery rhymes and stories	To gather, organise and classify literal, inferential and evaluative information in order to respond to questions. To skim and scan text to locate the same or similar meaning to key words in the questions.	✓	✓	✓	✓	✓	✓	✓

Chapter 1

Retelling

Introduction

Oral retelling is the best place to start with comprehension. Retelling is a key skill that reflects a child's comprehension of a text. To retell, children need to select the most important points from text and pictures and retell it in their own words – coherently, succinctly and in logical order. Summarising helps children to build an overall understanding of text or picture narratives, and also provides young children with a basic and familiar writing frame.

Poster notes

The story of the gingerbread man (page 9)
This poster introduces three key elements of a story to the children. Use the actions below to underpin the elements as you share them.
- Who – character (prompt: circle a hand around your face).
- What – action (prompt: run on the spot).
- Where – place (prompt: put a hand on your brow as though you are searching).

These are the three quick 'retelling' prompts that children need to locate before they can begin to retell a story.

In this chapter

	About the section	About the comprehension activity
Who, what, where? page 10	Children look at pictures and establish who is in them, what they are doing and where they are.	Children answer literal questions about an image from *My Perfect Pet* by Stuart Trotter.
Problem and resolution page 14	Children begin to think about problem and resolution within stories.	Children look at a photograph and infer meaning from it.
Retelling instructions page 18	Children consider the importance of sequence by looking at instructions.	Children look at an extract about making a pizza and answer questions about it that focus on sequencing.
Sequencing page 22	Looking at beginning, middle and end the children think about the structure of stories.	Children look at an extract that asks questions about the progressive stages of a frog's development.

Retelling

The story of the gingerbread man

Who, what, where?

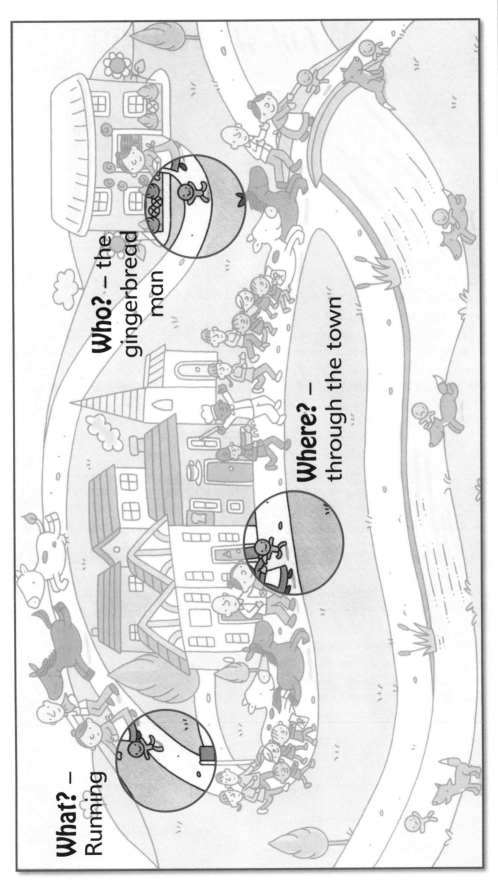

Who? – the gingerbread man

Where? – through the town

What? – Running

Illustrations © 2009, Cathy Hughes/Beehive Illustration.

Who, what, where?

To retell using key questions to highlight the main points of a story: *Who? What? Where?*

Background knowledge

Looking for 'who', 'what' and 'where' in a picture is a simple and effective way to introduce character, action and place within a picture. This is a natural comprehension device that pre-school children use frequently with their parents. This questioning helps children gain a better understanding of picture narrative and how to establish the main points of a story – for example, *Who is that? What are they doing? Where are they?*

However, although it is natural for children to raise these questions to support their own understanding of text and pictures from a very young age, they may not think to use these skills to recall or retell a story without first being shown how to.

Skills

Explain to the children that they will be practising how to gather the most important points from picture information and to retell a story in three easy steps.

- **Photocopiable page 11 'The gingerbread man'**
  - First, tell the children the story of 'The gingerbread man' using the pictures on the photocopiable sheet. Next, locate 'who', 'what' and 'where' information from the text.

- Hand out copies of the photocopiable sheet to pairs and ask the children to discuss the character, action and place in the first picture. Encourage them to draw a picture of the same scene to help them think carefully about the 'who', 'what' and 'where' information within the picture. Finally, ask them to retell the picture information to their partners. Remind them that they need to say *who* is in the picture, *what* they are doing and *where* they are.
- Write the sentence *The gingerbread man is running out of the kitchen* on the board. Discuss what it says and locate for the children: who ('the gingerbread man'), what ('is running'), where ('out of the kitchen'). Ask the children to draw an image for each of the three elements. This will help them to consolidate the meaning of 'who', 'what' and 'where' and remind them that it also guides the way to put simple sentences together when they answer questions about a story.
- Repeat this exercise with the other images in the story.

Comprehension

- **Photocopiable pages 12 and 13 'He's not too snappy'**
  - Hand out the first photocopiable sheet. Encourage the children to look at the picture. Read the text together.
  - Provide the children with the second photocopiable sheet. Explain that they need to choose the correct answer, tick the box next to it and then fill in the blanks in the sentences.

What's on the CD-ROM

On the CD-ROM you will find:
- Printable versions of all three photocopiable pages.
- Answers to 'He's not too snappy (2)'.
- Interactive version of 'The gingerbread man'.

Name:

Who, what, where?

The gingerbread man

■ Look at the picture below. Think about who is in the picture, what they are doing and where they are.

SCHOLASTIC
www.scholastic.co.uk   PHOTOCOPIABLE   **Scholastic Literacy Skills**
Comprehension: Years 1 and 2   **11**

Name:

Who, what, where?

He's not too snappy (1)

He's not too snappy...

Text and illustration © 2006, Stuart Trotter (Rockpool Children's Book).

Who, what, where?

He's not too snappy (2)

1. Who is in the bath?

A boy. ☐   A dinosaur. ☐   A girl. ☐

A _____ is in the bath.

2. What is the boy doing in the bath?

The boy is washing a teddy in the bath. ☐

The boy is washing a crocodile in the bath. ☐

The boy is _____

_____ in the bath.

3. Where is the teddy sitting?

Teddy is sitting on the floor. ☐

Teddy is sitting on the crocodile's nose. ☐

Teddy is sitting on _____

_____ .

4. Who is not too snappy?

_____

_____ is not too snappy.

Problem and resolution

Objective

To retell, extending the main 'who', 'what' and 'where' points of a story to include theme, conflict and resolution.

Background knowledge

Once a child can retell easily using basic character, action and place information, the summarising process can be extended. This will include: what the story is about (the theme); what the problem is for the character(s) (conflict); how the problem is eventually solved, what happens in the end (resolution). This process is helped along by showing children how to identify 'theme', 'problem' and 'solution' within picture narrative and text.

Skills

Explain to the children that the purpose of these activities is to show them how to gather more than just the 'who', 'what' and 'where' information in order to retell the whole story. They will be learning how to identify the problem and solution within the picture information and text. It would be helpful to also mention that not every story may have a solution to a problem (for example, 'Humpty Dumpty'!).

● **Photocopiable page 15 'What's the problem?'**
  ● Display the story 'Sam and the cakes' from the photocopiable sheet. Ask the children to look carefully at the pictures and text to find information that is repeated or linked to every picture and line of text. This will help them to identify the story theme (what the story is mainly about). As a class, agree that the story is mainly about Sam and the cakes.

● Hand out the photocopiable sheet to pairs of children, with the bottom row of pictures folded under to hide them. Ask the children to discuss and then circle the picture from 'Sam and the cakes' that highlights Sam's problem. They should then circle the box that shows the solution to his problem.
● Once the children have successfully done this, ask them to look at the row of pictures under the heading 'What is the problem?'. Ask the children to discuss what they think has gone wrong for the characters in each picture.
● Invite the children to unfold the bottom of the page to reveal the solution pictures. Ask them to draw a line joining the problem and resolution. Invite them to explain why they think these are solutions to the problems.
● Ask the children in pairs to retell the story of Sam to each other.

Comprehension

● **Photocopiable pages 16 and 17 'Football in the garden'**
  ● Hand out the first photocopiable sheet. Ask the children to look at the picture. Discuss what they think might be happening.
  ● Give the children the second photocopiable page. Ask the children to use the picture to help them answer the questions. They need to tick the box next to the correct answer and complete the sentence to show they can identify the problem in the picture and how it is resolved.

What's on the CD-ROM

On the CD-ROM you will find:
● Printable versions of all three photocopiable pages.
● Answers to 'What's the problem?' and 'Football in the garden (2)'.
● Interactive versions of 'What's the problem?' and 'Football in the garden'.

What's the problem?

■ Read the story below. Who and what is it about?

Sam and the cakes

Yum! Yum!	Oh no!	Oh yessss!	Mmmmh!
Sam can see some cakes.	Sam **can't** get the cakes.	Sam **can** get the cakes.	Sam loves cakes.

■ Look at the problems below. Unfold the bottom of the page. Draw a line from the problem to the solution.

What is the problem?

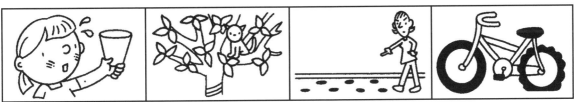

(fold)

The solution

Illustrations © 2009, Cathy Hughes/Beehive Illustration.

Name:

Football in the garden (1)

PHOTOCOPIABLE

Illustrations © 2009, Cathy Hughes/Beehive Illustration.

Problem and resolution

Football in the garden (2)

1. What game are the children playing?

Tennis ☐   Football ☐   Cricket ☐

The game the children are playing is

_____ .

2. Why did the game stop?

The game stopped because they were tired. ☐

The game stopped because they were bored. ☐

The game stopped because they lost the ball. ☐

The game stopped because _____

_____ .

3. What happened in the end?

In the end they didn't find their ball. ☐

In the end the man next door threw

their ball back. ☐

In the end they all went home for tea. ☐

In the end _____

_____ .

Retelling instructions

Objective

To organise non-fiction information and to retell it in the correct order.

Background knowledge

Young children need to know that instructions are made up of a series of small steps that need to be retold in the right order to show the listener how to complete a new task well. It is also important that young children understand that retelling non-fiction information must be done accurately and in the correct order so that it makes sense to the person listening.

Display the following sequencing guide to help the children:
To follow these instructions you must... First... Next... Then... Finally...

Skills

Explain to the children that the purpose of these activities is to show them how to repeat instructions accurately by putting the information in the right order.

● **Photocopiable page 19 'Jam sandwich'**
  ● First, ask the children if they already know how to make a jam sandwich. For those who know, ask them to retell to the class using the sequencing guide ('first', 'next', 'then').

● Hand out the photocopiable sheet and ask the children to cut out the pictures that show the different stages of making a jam sandwich. Explain that they should use the word cards to help put the pictures in the correct order but before they do, ask them to imagine that these will be instructions for someone else to follow. They need to arrange the pictures in the correct order so that the instructions make sense. When completed, ask them to retell the instructions.

● The children could draw their own sequence of images (for example, how they get ready for school in the morning) and label them with 'first', 'next', 'then' in a similar style to the photocopiable sheet.

Comprehension

● **Photocopiable pages 20 and 21 'Making a pizza'**
  ● Share the first photocopiable sheet. Look at the pictures and read the text together. Tell the children that they are instructions and ask them to think carefully about the order of them.
  ● Provide the children with copies of both photocopiable sheets. Remind them to refer to the text when they answer the questions.

 What's on the CD-ROM

On the CD-ROM you will find:
● Printable versions of all three photocopiable pages.
● Answers to 'Making a pizza (2)'.
● Interactive versions of 'Jam sandwich' and 'Making a pizza'.

Retelling instructions

Jam sandwich

■ Cut out the pictures and the labels below. Put them in the correct order.

First	Next	Then
Finally		

Illustrations © 2009, Cathy Hughes/Beehive Illustration.

SCHOLASTIC
www.scholastic.co.uk   **PHOTOCOPIABLE**   **Scholastic Literacy Skills**
Comprehension: Years 1 and 2   **19**

Name:

Retelling instructions

Making a pizza (1)

Dad makes a pizza base.

Dad puts the sauce on the pizza.

Dad puts the cheese on the pizza.

Dad puts the pizza in the oven.

Dad puts the pizza on the table.

Yum! Yum! The pizza is good!

PHOTOCOPIABLE **◼SCHOLASTIC**
www.scholastic.co.uk

Retelling instructions

Making a pizza (2)

1. Who makes the pizza?

Mum ☐	Children ☐	Dad ☐

2. What does Dad do first?

Dad puts the sauce on the pizza first.   ☐

Dad makes a pizza base first.   ☐

Dad _____ first.

3. What does Dad put on the pizza last?

Dad puts ham on the pizza last.   ☐

Dad puts grated cheese on the pizza last.   ☐

Dad puts _____ on the pizza last.

4. When Dad has made the pizza what does he do next?

Dad puts the pizza on the table next.   ☐

Dad puts the pizza in the oven next.   ☐

Dad puts the pizza _____ next.

Illustrations © 2009, Cathy Hughes/Beehive Illustration.

Sequencing

Objective

To organise story information and to retell it in sequence.

Background knowledge

Children need to know that story narratives that include characters, actions and events will probably have a problem and a resolution. The story will also have a beginning, middle and an end that is built around a sequence of events. It is important that the children are aware that others may not have heard the story before, so in order for them to follow what happens, they will need to hear the main points of the story in the order that they happen, starting from the beginning.

For young children to retell the main points of a story meaningfully they need to understand that the beginning introduces the characters (what they are doing and where they are); the middle describes what the problem is; and the end explains the solution to the problem.

To help children order their thoughts before retelling a fairly complex story, the following sequencing guide might be useful:
- **Beginning:** The story is about… (Who? What? Where?)
- **Middle:** The problem is that…
- **End:** What happens in the end is…

Skills

These activities help children to practise retelling the beginning, middle and end of a story in the right sequence of events.

- **Photocopiable page 23 'Incy Wincy Spider'**
  - As a class, say the rhyme 'Incy Wincy Spider'.
  - Hand out the photocopiable sheet and ask the children to look at the pictures. Can they use them to retell the rhyme as a story to their partners?
  - Discuss the difficulties their partners found understanding the retelling. Did it have a recognisable beginning, middle or end? Agree as a class that the images are in the wrong order. Ask the children to cut out the pictures and stick them in the correct order with the 'beginning', 'middle' and 'end' labels.
  - Ask them to retell the story to their partners using their pictures as a guide. Remind them of the sequencing guide above (and on the sheet) that will help them keep their story in order.

Comprehension

- **Photocopiable pages 24 and 25 'Tadpole to frog'**
  - Look at the first photocopiable sheet together. Discuss what the illustrations show. Ask children who have seen frogspawn or frogs to describe their experiences. Look at the sequence in which the stages occur and encourage the children to use the terms 'beginning', 'middle' and 'end'.
  - Provide the children with both photocopiable sheets. Ask them to use the text to answer the questions and complete the sentences. Remind them to think about the progression of 'beginning', 'middle' and 'end'.

What's on the CD-ROM

On the CD-ROM you will find:
- Printable versions of all three photocopiable pages.
- Answers to 'Tadpole to frog (2)'.
- Interactive version of 'Incy Wincy Spider'.

Sequencing

Incy Wincy Spider

■ Can you use the pictures to retell Incy Wincy Spider?

Down came the rain and washed the spider out. 	Out came the sunshine and dried up all the rain. 
Incy Wincy Spider climbed up the water spout. 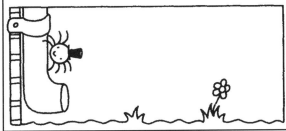	And Incy Wincy Spider climbed up the spout again. 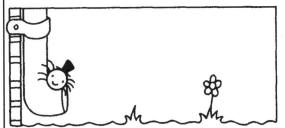

■ Cut out the pictures above and stick them in the correct order using the labels below.

Beginning	Middle
Middle	End

■ Retell the story in the right order to your partner.

Beginning: The story is about...

(Who? What? Where?)

Middle: The problem is that...

End: What happens in the end is...

Illustrations © 2009, Cathy Hughes/Beehive Illustration.

Name:

Sequencing

Tadpole to frog (1)

Frogspawn

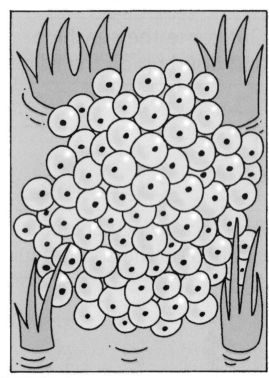

Tadpole

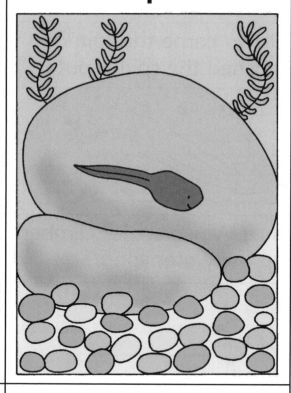

Tadpole with legs

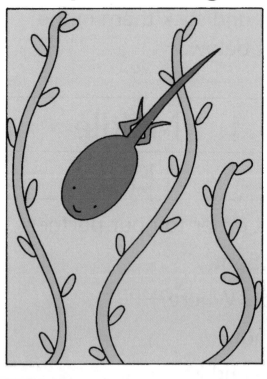

Frog

Sequencing

Tadpole to frog (2)

1. What does a frog look like at the start?

A frog only has a head and a tail at the start. ☐

A frog looks like a dot in some jelly at the start. ☐

The frog _____

_____ at the start.

2. When does a frog grow its legs?

A frog grows its legs in frogspawn. ☐

A frog grows its legs after it has a head and tail. ☐

The frog grows its legs _____

_____ .

3. What is a frog called when it is growing?

A frog is called frogspawn when it is growing. ☐

A frog is called a tadpole when it is growing. ☐

A frog is called _____

when it is growing.

4. When can the frog leave the water?

A frog can leave water when it is a tadpole. ☐

A frog can leave water when it is a frog. ☐

A frog can leave water when it is a _____ .

Chapter 2

Literal questioning

Introduction

Literal information is found directly on the page and does not require any interpretation to understand it. Literal questioning is the first of the three question types and is the primary source of information for very young children because it focuses on the characters, action and place that give the basic structure of a story.

Poster notes

Look and see the magic three! (page 27)
SeeBee, the literal bee, extracts literal information at a glance from pictures and text to provide himself with key information from which to ask and answer questions. It is useful to display the poster throughout Chapter 2 as it helps the children to grasp the concept of literal information. It also reminds them of how to identify and apply literal thinking when exploring other pictures and text.

In this chapter

	About the section	About the comprehension activity
'Who' questions page 28	Children ask and answer literal questions that focus on who the characters are.	Children answer 'who' questions about a picture from *Peace at Last* by Jill Murphy.
'What' questions page 32	Moving from 'who' to 'what', children answer literal questions about what characters are doing.	Children answer questions about a photograph of a vet.
'Where' questions page 36	Children focus on where the characters are in pictures.	*Cops and Robbers* by Janet and Allan Ahlberg provides the setting for this 'where' comprehension.
'Who', 'what' and 'where' questions page 40	Children consolidate 'who', 'what' and 'where' by looking at them all together.	A snowman photograph provides a rich environment to answer 'who', 'what' and 'where' questions.

Literal questioning

Look and see the magic three!

Can you help SeeBee work out who, what and where in the picture?

SeeBee can look and see. He can see the magic three:

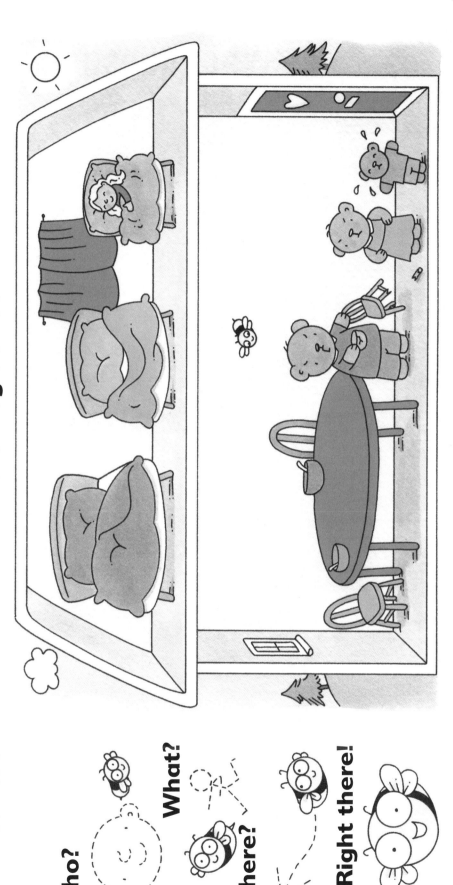

Who?

What?

Where?

Right there!

Illustrations © 2009, Cathy Hughes/Beehive Illustration.

'Who' questions

To identify literal information about characters within pictures. To gather, organise and classify this information to respond to and formulate questions.

Background knowledge

A good place to start comprehension is to work with 'who' questions as a whole class, identifying who the main character is, using pictures and text.

This is the easiest of the literal questions to recognise and respond to and answers can be checked quickly, because the character's identity replaces the 'who' word at the start of the question – the remainder of the sentence remains unchanged to give a full answer.

Remind the children that literal 'who' information is right there in the pictures or text for them to see.

Skills

Explain to the children that these activities will show them how to find information that will help them to ask and answer 'who' questions.

- **Photocopiable page 29 'Asking who questions'**
  - First, talk to the children about the purpose of questions.
  - Show them the difference between a statement (something you know), such as *Jade has a dog* and a question, *Who has a dog?*
  - Explain to them how placing 'who' at the beginning of the statement and adding a question mark at the end creates a question.

- Model this further by providing 'who' and a question mark on cards. Use these to help the children practise asking 'who' questions from a statement that also provides the answer.
- Hand out the photocopiable sheet. Ask the children to cut out the 'who' words and paste them over the girl's name at the front of the statements. Then paste the question mark at the end to make a question. Ask them to write the answer.
- Ask the children to make up their own 'who' questions from the SeeBee poster about Goldilocks, for example: *Who is asleep in Baby Bear's bed?* They can use the photocopiable sheet as a guide.

Comprehension

- **Photocopiable pages 30 and 31 'Peace at last'**
  - Hand out both photocopiable sheets to the children. To help them to complete the task more easily, ask the children to gather literal information about the characters in the picture before looking at the questions.
  - Once they have done this, ask them to answer the questions given and finally generate and answer their own 'who' question.

What's on the CD-ROM

On the CD-ROM you will find:
- Printable versions of all three photocopiable pages.
- Answers to 'Asking who questions' and 'Peace at last (2)'.
- Interactive versions of 'Asking who questions' and 'Peace at last'.

Asking who questions

■ Cut out the **who** and the question mark cards below. Make the questions into **who** questions. The first one has been done for you.
■ Write the answers to the questions.

Question: | Who | has lots of pets | ? |

Answer: **Jade** has lots of pets**.**

Question: | Jade | has a dog | . |

Answer: Jade has a dog.

Question: | Jade | has a snake | . |

Answer: _____

Question: | Jade | has a cat | . |

Answer: _____

| Who | Who | Who | ? | ? | ? |

Illustrations © 2009, Cathy Hughes/Beehive Illustration.

Name:

'Who' questions

Peace at last (1)

Illustration © 1980, 1995, 2007 Jill Murphy.

PHOTOCOPIABLE

'Who' questions

Peace at last (2)

1. Who is wearing pyjamas?

Father Bear [ ]	Mother Bear [ ]	Baby Bear [ ]

2. Who is asleep?

Father Bear is asleep. [ ]

Mother and Baby Bear are asleep. [ ]

_____ asleep.

3. Who is *not* asleep?

_____ is not asleep.

4. Who is yawning?

Father Bear is yawning. [ ]

Baby Bear is yawning. [ ]

_____ is yawning.

5. Your question:

Who _____

Your answer: _____

_____ .

Illustrations © 2009, Cathy Hughes/Beehive Illustration.

'What' questions

Objectives

To identify literal information about what the characters are doing within pictures. To gather, organise and classify this information in order to respond to questions and formulate own questions.

Background knowledge

'What' questions are more varied to ask and answer than 'who' questions. This is because in addition to the characters' actions, 'what' also asks about objects and events within a story.

Initially, show children how to ask and answer questions that focus on characters' actions and on objects within a story. These questions only require a verb or noun answer, whereas *What is happening in the story?* needs more information (a combination of 'who', 'what' and 'where') to give a full response.

Unlike 'who' questions where a proper noun simply replaces 'who' at the beginning or end of the sentence to give an answer, 'what' questions are only a partial guide for a response, as the words need to be rearranged to make a statement – for example: *What is he doing in the garden? He is running in the garden.*

Skills

Explain to the children that these activities will show them how to find information that will help them to ask and answer 'what' questions.

- **Photocopiable page 33 'Asking what questions'**
  - First, talk to the children about the difference between 'who' and 'what' questions. Then show them the difference between a statement (something you know) – for example, *Jo is singing* – and a 'what' question, *What is Jo doing?*

- Explain to them that when you need to know what someone is doing or what an object is, you need to ask 'what' at the beginning of the question.
- In pairs, ask one child to pretend to be either asleep or eating. Their partner must ask them *What are you doing?* and they need to respond with a full answer – either *I am sleeping* or *I am eating*.
- Ask them to take turns to ask 'what' questions in response to miming other actions.
- Hand out the photocopiable sheet and ask the children to complete the answers to the questions using the picture information.
- Next, ask them to cut out and reassemble the words in the box at the foot of the sheet in the correct order to put together the questions they answered above.
- Ask the children to make up their own 'what' questions using the SeeBee poster picture.

Comprehension

- **Photocopiable pages 34 and 35 'Visit to the vet'**
  - Show the children the picture and ask them to talk about the characters' actions, and about the objects in the picture.
  - Hand out both photocopiable sheets and ask the children to answer the literal 'what' questions and, finally, generate and answer their own question.

What's on the CD-ROM

On the CD-ROM you will find:
- Printable versions of all three photocopiable pages.
- Answers to 'Asking what questions' and 'Visit to the vet (2)'.
- Interactive version of 'Asking what questions'.

'What' questions

Asking what questions

- Write the missing word to complete the answer to the question. Use the pictures to help you.
- The first one has been done for you.

Question: What is the girl doing?

Answer: The girl is **eating**.

Question: What is the girl doing?

Answer: The girl is _____ .

Question: What is the cat doing?

Answer: The cat is _____ .

- Cut out the boxes below and arrange them into a question and answer.

What	is	the cat	doing
The cat	is	sleeping.	?

Illustrations © 2009, Cathy Hughes/Beehive Illustration.

Name:

Visit to the vet (1)

'What' questions

Photograph © Corbis Premium RF / Alamy.

PHOTOCOPIABLE

'What' questions

Visit to the vet (2)

1. What is the dog lying on?

The dog is lying on a bed. ☐

The dog is lying on a table. ☐

The dog is lying on _____ .

2. What is the vet doing to the dog?

The vet is stroking the dog. ☐

The vet is looking in the dog's ear. ☐

The vet is _____

_____ .

3. What is the man doing?

The man is holding the dog's leg. ☐

The man is holding the boy's hand. ☐

The man is holding _____ .

4. Your question:

What _____

Your answer: _____

_____ .

'Where' questions

Objectives

To identify literal information about where the characters are within pictures. To gather, organise and classify this information in order to respond to and formulate questions.

Background knowledge

After working with the complexities of answering 'what' questions, young children find it is much easier to answer questions that identify places and settings within pictures and text. Like 'what' questions, when they ask a 'where' question, the subject of the enquiry is usually at the end of a question (for example, *Where is Tom?*). To respond they simply need to begin their answer with the person's name, pronoun or noun and add the 'where' information at the end: *Tom is in bed.* Remind them that literal information about settings and the characters' whereabouts are right there in the picture information or text for them to see.

Skills

Explain to the children that these activities will show them how to find information that will help them to ask and answer literal 'where' questions.

- **Photocopiable page 37 'Hide and seek'**
  - Talk to the children about the difference between 'who', 'what' and 'where' questions. Give them an example of a literal 'where' question and answer, and compare the structure to a 'what' question and answer, such as: *Where is Tom? Tom is in bed. What is Tom doing? Tom is snoring.*

- Explain to the children that, when you need to know where someone is in the story, you need to ask 'where' at the beginning of the question. The information that gives the answer to the question is right there in the story.
- Hand out the photocopiable sheet. Ask the children to look at the picture and then to cut out the words at the bottom of the page to make 'where' questions and answers.
- Ask them to generate their own question and answer.
- Ask the children to make up their own 'where' questions using the SeeBee poster picture (for example, *Where is Goldilocks?*). They can use the photocopiable sheet as a guide.

Comprehension

- **Photocopiable pages 38 and 39 'Cops and robbers'**
  - Show the children the picture and ask them to talk about where the characters and objects are.
  - Provide them with both photocopiable pages. Ask them to answer the literal questions and, finally, to generate and answer their own 'where' question.

What's on the CD-ROM

On the CD-ROM you will find:
- Printable versions of all three photocopiable pages.
- Answers to 'Hide and seek' and 'Cops and robbers (2)'.
- Interactive versions of 'Hide and seek' and 'Cops and robbers'.

'Where' questions

Hide and seek

■ Cut out the questions and answers from the bottom of the page.

■ Match each question with its answer. Use the picture to help you.

Where is the girl?	The boy is under the bed.
Where is the boy?	The book is on the bed.
Where is the book?	The girl is behind the door.

Illustrations © 2009, Cathy Hughes/Beehive Illustration.

Name:

Cops and robbers (1)

Illustration © 1977, Janet Ahlberg.

PHOTOCOPIABLE

'Where' questions

Cops and robbers (2)

1. Where are the robbers?

The garden ☐	The house ☐	The garage ☐

The robbers are _____ .

2. Where are the family?

The family are on holiday. ☐

The family are in bed asleep. ☐

The family are _____ .

3. Where is the robber digging?

The robber is digging in the garden. ☐

The robber is digging under the house. ☐

The robber is digging in the sandpit. ☐

The robber is digging _____

_____ .

4. Your question:

Where _____

Your answer: _____ .

Illustrations © 2009, Cathy Hughes/Beehive Illustration.

'Who', 'what' and 'where' questions

Objectives

To identify literal key word information about characters, action and place within text. To gather, organise and classify this information in order to respond to and formulate questions.

Background knowledge

Once children can generate and answer 'who', 'what' and 'where' literal questions from pictures with ease, show them how to ask and answer literal questions from text. When authors write, they have a picture in their heads that they want to pass on to their readers. To do this they select a subject their readers know something about and choose words carefully to describe what is in their head. These create the main points of the story, the literal 'who', 'what' and 'where' information, and they paint the picture for the reader. The author wants to put the reader in the story so they can see who is involved, what they are doing, what is happening and where they are.

Remind the children that questions usually begin with 'who', 'what' or 'where' and that the literal information and answers are right there in the text.

Skills

Explain to the children that these activities will show them how to gather 'who', 'what' and 'where' information correctly in order to ask and answer literal questions from text and pictures.

- **Photocopiable page 41 'A pig rolling in the mud'**
  - Give the children an example of how words paint pictures in their heads (for example, a sandcastle). Ask them to take it in turns to say an object that will give the other children a picture in their heads.

- Explain that if they don't get a picture in their heads when they read or hear a word they probably do not understand the meaning of the word and need to find out.
- Write *The cat sat on the mat* on the board. Ask the children to draw a picture of the sentence. Did they all draw a cat sitting on a mat? Did the words give them a picture in their heads to draw from? Highlight 'cat' (who), 'sat' (what) and 'mat' (where) and explain that you can ask questions from this key word information.
- Hand out the photocopiable sheet and ask the children to firstly label the image and then write the correct 'who', 'what', 'where' information in the columns from the picture. Then ask them to complete the 'who', 'what' and 'where' questions using the correct question word. Finally, ask them to generate their own questions and answers from the picture.

Comprehension

- **Photocopiable pages 42 and 43 'Making a snowman'**
  - Hand out both photocopiable sheets. Suggest that the children highlight the characters, action and place within the line of text before they look at the questions.
  - Ask them to use this information to help them to accurately answer the literal questions and ask and answer their own question from the text.

What's on the CD-ROM

On the CD-ROM you will find:
- Printable versions of all three photocopiable pages.
- Answers to 'A pig rolling in the mud' and 'Making a snowman (2)'.
- Interactive versions of 'A pig rolling in the mud' and 'Making a snowman'.

'Who', 'what' and 'where' questions

A pig rolling in the mud

■ Label the picture with the words in the box.

pig	rolling	mud	sheep	field
chasing	sheepdog	birds	flying	sky

■ Put the key words from the picture in the right columns.

Who	What (doing)	Where
pig	rolling	mud

■ Write a **who**, **what** or **where** question below.

_____

_____

Illustrations © 2009, Cathy Hughes/Beehive Illustration.

Name:

Making a snowman (1)

Photograph © Blend Images / Alamy.

The two boys are making a snowman in the woods.

PHOTOCOPIABLE   ■SCHOLASTIC
www.scholastic.co.uk

'Who', 'what' and 'where' questions

Making a snowman (2)

1. Who is making a snowman?

Two boys are making a snowman. ☐

A girl is making a snowman. ☐

_____ making a snowman.

2. What are the snowman's arms made from?

The snowman's arms are made from snow. ☐

The snowman's arms are made from sticks. ☐

The snowman's arms are made from _____

3. Where are the boys?

The boys are at home. ☐

The boys are in the woods. ☐

The boys are _____ .

4. Write your own question from the text:

_____

_____

Your answer: _____

_____ .

Chapter 3

Prediction

Introduction

Prediction is a key skill in comprehension. Through self-questioning, reasoning and seeking clues that are connected to the author's intention and to their own experience, children learn to logically anticipate what will happen next and to justify their predictions. This chapter focuses on asking children to use the information in front of them to make informed predictions about what comes next, what a story might be about, and what signs and symbols mean.

Poster notes

Pam the powerful predictor (page 45)
Pam the powerful predictor is a useful analogy to help children grasp the tricky concept of foretelling. The poster presents familiar information about a well-known nursery rhyme that suggests a different ending from the traditional story. It is important that children understand that when Pam makes guesses about what may have happened before or after in a story, she always gives the clues that explain her prediction.

In this chapter

	About the section	About the comprehension activity
What happens next? page 46	Children gather information from images that suggest the reasons for why things happen or might happen.	Children answer literal questions about *Eating Out* by Helen Oxenbury and then they predict the outcome.
Rhythm and rhyme page 50	This section looks at the importance of rhythm and rhyme for children's comprehension.	Children write, or cut and paste, words to complete 'Three little ducks'.
Clues from the cover page 54	Book covers are the focus here. They are key in prediction, helping children to glean a lot of information on characters, events and so on.	Children use the information on a book cover to answer questions about it.
Reading signs and symbols page 58	Gathering information from pictures and symbols that inform, warn and instruct.	Children look at pictures which include symbols, and answer questions about them.

Prediction

Pam the powerful predictor

Illustrations © 2009, Cathy Hughes/Beehive Illustration.

What happens next?

To find clues from images that suggest what might happen next.

Background knowledge

When young children are able to recognise how actions or events produce certain results, they are able to predict story and non-fiction outcomes. It is useful for them to understand the thinking, questioning and reasoning involved in this process: that when they predict, they are linking prior knowledge and personal experience to clues given by the author to calculate what happened before or what will happen next.

To help children to meaningfully and logically anticipate consequences for characters and events in fiction and non-fiction, it is necessary for them to participate in as much 'think-aloud' talk as possible to work through the likely progression of events. This will help them to make the necessary links that explain how cause and effect works – for example: *If a character takes this action this might happen because…* or *If this has happened what must have happened before is this because…*

Skills

Explain to the children that these activities will show them how to predict what will happen next to characters, settings and key events in a story narrative or non-fiction picture.

- **Photocopiable page 47 'What goes up…'**
  - Talk to the children about the purpose of prediction and how some actions have outcomes that can be anticipated. For example: *If you jump up you will come back down again.*

- Discuss everyday cause and effect situations and encourage the children to talk about examples of things that have happened to them because of their actions. For example, if you catch a child speaking in class they might be told off.
- Hand out the photocopiable sheet. Talk about the actions shown on the page and ask the children to draw a line to the possible outcomes.
- Ask pairs to talk about the picture at the bottom of the photocopiable sheet. What clues in the picture warn them of what may happen next? Ask them to draw what they think will be the outcome.

Comprehension

- **Photocopiable pages 48 and 49 'Eating out'**
  - Hand out both photocopiable pages. Encourage the children to talk about the picture in pairs. What do they think is happening?
  - Then, ask them to answer the questions. When they have completed the sheet, you might want to encourage them to draw a picture of what they think will happen next, and ask them to explain why they think that.

What's on the CD-ROM

On the CD-ROM you will find:
- Printable versions of all three photocopiable pages.
- Answers to 'What goes up…' and 'Eating out (2)'.
- Interactive versions of 'What goes up…' and 'Eating out'.

What happens next?

What goes up...

■ Look at the pictures below. Can you draw a line to show what might have happened next?

Action	**Possible outcomes**

■ What might happen next in this picture?

Name:

Eating out (1)

Illustration © 1983, Helen Oxenbury.

What happens next?

Eating out (2)

1. Who is sitting at the table?

A man is sitting at the table. ☐

A lady and two children are sitting at the table. ☐

_____ are sitting at the table.

2. What is happening in the picture?

The table is falling over. ☐

The waiter and the boy are falling over. ☐

The _____ falling over.

3. What is the cause of the trouble in the picture?

The waiter   Someone tripping   Someone falling

 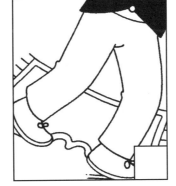 

The cause of the trouble is _____ .

4. What will happen next? Draw a picture on the back of this sheet. You answer:

_____

_____ .

■SCHOLASTIC
www.scholastic.co.uk   **PHOTOCOPIABLE**   **Scholastic Literacy Skills**
Comprehension: Years 1 and 2   **49**

Rhythm and rhyme

Objective

To look for clues in text and pictures that suggest what might happen next.

Background knowledge

Predicting is a strategy that young children enjoy because it requires them to make personal links with the author's intention and to think ahead logically as they read. It helps them to monitor their reading comprehension and to look for context clues to support their understanding of unknown words within text.

Rhyme provides young children with the perfect opportunity, in the early stages of learning to read, to practise prediction skills effectively. The strong rhythm, and repetitive words and phrases that rhyme offers, build children's confidence in reading and encourage them to anticipate the last word or next line correctly.

Skills

Explain to the children that these activities will show them how to anticipate and predict what will happen next to characters, settings and key events from clues in text and pictures.

- **Photocopiable page 51 'Pat's rhyming box'**
  - Talk to the children about how predicting asks them to think ahead and guess what might happen next, using clues from pictures and text on the page to guide them.

- Talk about how rhyming words can help them to predict words that may come next and how important it is for them to say the rhyme aloud. Explain that this helps them to 'hear' the rhythm and anticipate the words that are coming at the end of each line.
- Remind the children that the rhyming words they anticipate need to make sense to help tell the story of the rhyme.
- Hand out the photocopiable sheet and ask the children to look at the picture at the top of the page and say what rhyming items are in Pat's box.
- Ask them to write down the missing word at the end of each line and draw a picture that refers to one of the items in Pat's box.

Comprehension

- **Photocopiable pages 52 and 53 'Three little ducks'**
  - Read the rhyme from the first photocopiable sheet aloud with the children. Ask them to identify any rhyming words.
  - Provide the children with the second photocopiable sheet and ask them to either cut and paste the missing words or write them in the spaces. Give the children the first photocopiable sheet if they are struggling with the missing words.

What's on the CD-ROM

On the CD-ROM you will find:
- Printable versions of all three photocopiable pages.
- Answers to 'Pat's rhyming box' and 'Three little ducks (2)'.
- Interactive version of 'Three little ducks'.

Rhythm and rhyme

Pat's rhyming box

- Look at what Pat has in his box.
- Write the name of each item below to create a rhyme. Draw a picture of the object in the box.

Look, Pat has a

_____

Look, Pat has a

_____

Look, Pat has a

_____

Look, Pat has a

_____

Look, Pat has a

_____

Illustrations © 2009, Cathy Hughes/Beehive Illustration.

PHOTOCOPIABLE

Name:

Three little ducks (1)

Three little ducks went swimming one day,

Over the pond and far away.

Mummy duck said "Quack, quack, quack".

But only two little ducks came swimming back.

Two little ducks went swimming one day,

Over the pond and far away.

Mummy duck said "Quack, quack, quack".

But only one little duck came swimming back.

One little duck went swimming one day,

Over the pond and far away.

Mummy duck said "Quack, quack, quack".

But no little ducks came swimming back.

Mummy duck went swimming one day,

Over the pond and far away.

Mummy duck said "Quack, quack, quack".

And all the little ducks came swimming back!

Illustrations © 2009, Cathy Hughes/Beehive Illustration.

Rhythm and rhyme

Three little ducks (2)

■ Fill in the missing words from the bottom of the page.

Three little ducks went swimming one day,

Over the pond and _____ .

Mummy duck said "Quack, quack, quack".

But only two little ducks came swimming _____ .

Two little _____ went swimming one day,

Over the pond and far _____ .

Mummy duck said "Quack, quack, quack".

But only one little duck came swimming back.

_____ little duck went swimming one day,

_____ .

Mummy duck said _____ .

But _____ came swimming back.

One	away	back	far away
Over the pond and far away			ducks
"Quack, quack, quack"		no little ducks	

Clues from the cover

Objective

To show how to look for clues in pictures and the title of a book to predict what to expect from the story or information inside.

Background knowledge

An essential device for engaging young children's initial interest in a story or non-fiction book is to discuss the cover information and what it suggests about the contents inside. A cover will convey to the reader whether the book is fiction or non-fiction. From the title and pictures the children will see whether it is a theme or subject they already know about and the sort of vocabulary they may need to know. The book title often provides key word clues about the contents and theme of the book, whereas the cover picture tends to offer more inferred information about the characters and events inside. The clues from the imagery help to further stimulate the reader's interest and encourage them to make more detailed predictions about the story or information inside.

Skills

Explain to the children that these activities will show them how to anticipate story narrative or non-fiction subject matter from clues given in titles and pictures.

- **Photocopiable page 55 'Book covers'**
  - Show the children examples of fiction and non-fiction covers and talk about the differences between them. Explain that the title and picture on the cover offers clues about the book's contents inside.

- Non-fiction book titles tend to offer literal key information about the contents and often have photographs about the subject matter on the cover.
- By contrast, story books usually rely on the illustrations to suggest what the story narrative is about and key word clues in the title to indicate the story theme.
- Hand out the photocopiable sheet and ask the children to first tick the book they think is non-fiction and explain why.
- Ask pairs to highlight the key words in the titles and talk about what they think the books might be about from this information.
- From the clues given in the titles, ask them to cut and paste the cover picture they think best fits the two books.
- Ask them to choose from the two book titles and draw their own picture of what they think the book is about – using 'who', 'what', 'where' as a guide.

Comprehension

- **Photocopiable pages 56 and 57 'Has anyone here seen William?'**
  - Display the first photocopiable page and ask the children to discuss the cover image. Ask them to discuss what the book might be about with a partner.
  - Hand out both photocopiable pages and ask the children to answer the questions about the cover.

 What's on the CD-ROM

On the CD-ROM you will find:
- Printable versions of all three photocopiable pages.
- Answers to 'Book covers' and 'Has anyone here seen William? (2)'.
- Interactive versions of 'Book covers' and 'Has anyone here seen William?'.

Clues from the cover

Book covers

■ Look at the book covers below. Which do you think is the non-fiction book? Why do you think that?

Non-fiction ☐

Non-fiction ☐

■ Read the title for the books. Cut and paste one image for each cover from those below.

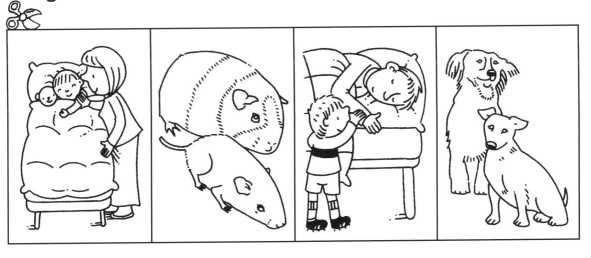

Illustrations © 2009, Cathy Hughes/Beehive Illustration.

Name:

Has anyone here seen William? (1)

Illustration © 1988, Blackbird Design Pty Ltd.

SCHOLASTIC
www.scholastic.co.uk

Clues from the cover

Has anyone here seen William? (2)

1. What sort of book do you think this is?

Fiction (story book)   ☐

Non-fiction (information book)   ☐

2. Why do you say this?

It has a photo and information in the title that
tells me what it is about.   ☐

It has a drawing of characters and part of a
story scene on the cover.   ☐

3. Who is this book about?

This book is about Bob Graham.   ☐

This book is about William.   ☐

This book is about ducks.   ☐

This book is about _____ .

4. What do you think the story is about?

The story is about a boy feeding ducks at a pond. ☐

The story is about the search for William.   ☐

The story is about _____

_____ .

Reading signs and symbols

Objective

To predict warning, information and instruction from picture symbols and signs.

Background knowledge

At home or out in the community, generic pictures and symbols are a familiar part of our daily lives. They provide instant warning, information and instruction using few words. They are particularly useful for early readers, as their simple bold picture silhouettes and symbolic shapes are usually a logical replacement for the written word and are generally easy to interpret. With adult support, young children are able to understand and remember the meaning of many of these symbols.

By relying on similar interpretation and prediction devices used to comprehend picture stories, children are capable of understanding and responding to many of the everyday symbols and signs around them (for example, a heart for love, a man or woman for toilets). In addition to general information, many signs also prompt them to consider what may happen to their personal safety or the welfare of others if they ignore the warning and instruction being offered.

Skills

Explain to the children that these activities will show them how to predict the meaning from key clues in pictures and symbols.

- **Photocopiable page 65 'Signs'**
  - Explain to the children that information signs around them at home and in the outside world are there to help them, to keep them safe and to guide them.

- Talk about how images can suggest something without words. Tell the children that symbols for feelings, actions, occupations, events and so on are often represented by simple drawings of objects that are linked to these things in some way.
- Hand out the photocopiable sheet and ask the children to talk in pairs about the meaning of each picture symbol and to write the words that match the pictures from the list of words given.
- Explain that symbols are also displayed as signs that warn, inform or instruct you (for example, weather forecast symbols).
- Ask pairs to work out what they think the signs mean in these categories – what do they think might happen if they or others ignored the warning or instruction signs?
- Finally, tell them to draw their own symbol or sign for their partner to see if they can guess the meaning.

Comprehension

- **Photocopiable pages 66 or 67 'Weather map'**
  - Hand out the first photocopiable sheet. Ask the children to look at and discuss the pictures.
  - Then ask them to answer the questions and complete the sentences on the second photocopiable sheet.

 What's on the CD-ROM

On the CD-ROM you will find:
- Printable versions of all three photocopiable pages.
- Answers to 'Signs' and 'Weather map (2)'.

Reading signs and symbols

Signs

■ What do these symbols mean? Match the words with the picture meaning.

Happy   Love   Magic   Time

■ What do these signs mean?

Warning signs	Information signs	Instruction signs
(children crossing triangle sign)	(toilet, disabled, baby changing signs)	(bicycle in circle sign)
(falling rocks triangle sign)	(seesaw diamond sign)	(no diving circle sign)

Name:

Weather map (1)

It will be rainy.

Illustration © 1996, Mal Peet.

PHOTOCOPIABLE

Reading signs and symbols

Weather map (2)

1. What is the man doing in the picture?

The man is giving a weather forecast. ☐

The man is standing in the rain. ☐

The man is _____

_____ .

2. What do the cloud symbols mean on the map?

The cloud symbols mean it is going to be windy. ☐

The cloud symbols mean it is going to be rainy. ☐

The cloud symbols mean it is going to be sunny. ☐

The cloud symbols mean _____

_____ .

3. What would the symbols on the map be if the boy was making a snowman in the picture?

Symbol of sun  ☐

Symbol of rain  ☐

Symbol of snow cloud  ☐

Chapter 4

Inference

Introduction

This chapter moves on to look at 'how' and 'why'. The children are shown how to search for clues using prediction skills to understand the author's hidden and implied meaning in order to answer and generate their own questions. They are shown how authors encourage readers to infer extra details. Like a detective, they learn how to delve deeper for evidence to back up what they have inferred from pictures and text. This procedure also helps them to identify the difference between being literal and using inference to gather information in order to ask and answer questions.

This process significantly improves the children's vocabulary, helps them to make key links, and encourages independent reasoning and deduction.

Poster notes

Duggie Dog the text detective (page 63)
The poster offers an analogy and progressive picture guide to support inference questioning: Detective Duggie Dog shows the children that they can dig deeper into a story than SeeBee the literal bee, who is only able to see 'who', 'what', 'where' at the surface of a story. Duggie Dog can also ask 'when', 'why' and 'how' to uncover the author's intentions and meaning from clues on the page. He always gives reasons for his deductions from the clues he finds.

The poster is a useful classroom aid that reminds children of the thinking involved in inferential enquiry.

In this chapter

	About the section	About the comprehension activity
Seeking meaning page 64	Identifying inferred information from an image.	Children look at *The Blue Balloon* by Mick Inkpen and answer questions about inferred picture information.
Finding clues page 68	Gathering inferred information and evidence from picture narrative and text.	Children study an image from *Smelly Jelly Smelly Fish* by Michael Rosen and infer meaning from it.
Presenting evidence page 72	Using the word 'because' to explain something has been inferred.	Studying a photograph, children infer meaning from it and explain why they think this.
How I know page 76	Children begin to ask and answer their own inference questions with reasons.	Studying images from *Father Christmas* by Raymond Briggs, children infer meaning and write their own questions.

Inference

DUGGIE DOG THE TEXT DETECTIVE

Illustrations © 2009, Cathy Hughes/Beehive Illustration.

Seeking meaning

Objective

To identify and interpret inferred meaning from picture clues to better understand the author's intention.

Background knowledge

When children have asked all the literal questions they can from pictures and text, they naturally move on to a deeper level for inferred information (without knowing it!). These activities show them how to recognise when they are using these skills, so they can intentionally locate and interpret implied and hidden meaning within picture information by asking questions. They are introduced to picture narrative first because it helps them to infer from text with greater ease later on and offers a teaching approach that is accessible for children of all reading abilities. Young children are shown how to identify and understand word clues in an inference question that link to inferred clues in the picture information to give the answer. They are also reminded that good detectives always provide evidence from the information given to explain their deductions.

Skills

Explain to the children that these activities will show them how to find clues that will help them to give reasoned answers to inference questions about picture narrative.

- **Photocopiable page 65 'Every picture tells a story'**
  - Talk with the children about the difference between being literal and using inference.
  - Explain that when they can no longer ask 'who', 'what', 'where' questions from what they can see right there on the page, they need to look deeper for information that is only suggested.

- Explain that inferred clues hint at meaning and ask you to make connections between other information in the picture and your own knowledge. They also require you to prove how you know.
- Hand out the photocopiable sheet and ask the children to look carefully at the picture in the centre of the page and talk in pairs about the literal 'who', 'what', 'where' information they can see.
- Now ask them to think about clues in the picture that they cannot see. What questions could they ask to explain what is happening or may happen next? What clues can they find that they can predict from? For example: *Why is mum holding her hat on? What might happen next?*
- Ask them in their pairs to draw a line that links each picture clue to part of the main picture and explain how they know.

Comprehension

- **Photocopiable pages 66 and 67 'The blue balloon'**
  - To answer the inference questions from the pictures more easily, ask the children to first look at the illustrations and think and search for clues that suggest what is happening in each picture and why.
  - Once they have done this they can move on to answer the questions.

What's on the CD-ROM

On the CD-ROM you will find:
- Printable versions of all three photocopiable pages.
- Answers to 'The blue balloon (2)'.
- Interactive version of 'The blue balloon'.

Seeking meaning

Every picture tells a story

■ Look at the big picture. Can you link the pictures around the outside to something in the main picture. The first one has been done for you.

Fish   Kite   Towel

Sandwiches   Wind   Sandcastle   Bottle of drink

Name:

The blue balloon (1)

Illustration © 1989, Mick Inkpen.

Scholastic Literacy Skills
Comprehension: Years 1 and 2

PHOTOCOPIABLE

SCHOLASTIC
www.scholastic.co.uk

Seeking meaning

The blue balloon (2)

1. What is happening to the boy and his dog?

They are floating up into the sky. ☐

They are falling from the sky. ☐

2. How do you know that?

I know that because they are passing flying

birds and are floating up to the stars. ☐

I know that because the boy is holding on to

the dog tightly. ☐

3. Have they been floating for a long time?

Yes, they have been floating for a long time. ☐

No, they haven't been floating for a long time. ☐

4. How do you know that?

I know that because it is getter dark and the

stars are out. ☐

I know that because they don't look tired. ☐

They _____

because _____

_____ .

SCHOLASTIC
www.scholastic.co.uk   **PHOTOCOPIABLE**   Scholastic Literacy Skills
Comprehension: Years 1 and 2   **67**

Finding clues

Objective

To identify and interpret inferred meaning from text clues and pictures in order to respond to questions.

Background knowledge

These activities build on what the children have learned about inference in the previous section. It shows them how to:
● search for word and picture clues that infer the author's meaning and intention;
● gather evidence from these suggested and hidden clues to support their deductions.
    It may be helpful to refer the children again to the poster on page 63, 'Duggie Dog the text detective', to remind them that they can delve deeper to find answers to inference questions than SeeBee, the literal bee who can only see what is 'right there'.

Skills

Explain to the children that these activities will show them how to find clues that will help them to give reasoned answers to inference questions about non-fiction pictures and text.
● **Photocopiable page 69 'Can't go in'**
   ● Explain that authors and illustrators use clues that hint at meaning within text and pictures to make the writing more interesting.
   ● The clues they introduce ask you to think and search for connections between the information given (key words and images) and your own knowledge, in order to infer meaning and make deductions.

● Explain that when a detective infers from these clues and makes deductions he is also able to provide evidence to prove 'how he knows'.
● Read the text on the photocopiable sheet aloud to the children and ask them to talk in pairs about who it might be about, what the problem might be, where it might be happening and why.
● Hand out the photocopiable sheet. Ask the children to follow the examples given and highlight the clue words in the sentences that infer an answer to these questions.
● Ask the children to search the picture for key information that links to the word clues and provides evidence to support their answers.
● Ask them to draw a line from the text clues to the clues in the picture and talk about why they think these clues link.

Comprehension

● **Photocopiable pages 70 and 71 'Smelly Jelly Smelly Fish'**
   ● Ask the children to search for clues to explain what is happening in the scene on the first photocopiable sheet.
   ● Ask them to highlight the clues in the questions on the second photocopiable sheet to help them to respond accurately. Then ask them to answer the questions.

What's on the CD-ROM

On the CD-ROM you will find:
● Printable versions of all three photocopiable pages.
● Answers to 'Can't go in' and 'Smelly Jelly Smelly Fish (2)'.
● Interactive versions of 'Can't go in' and 'Smelly Jelly Smelly Fish'.

Name:

Can't go in

■ Link the word clues to the picture information. Who is the poem about?
What is the problem? Where is it happening? Remember to say how you know.

Can't go in

I can't go in – won't go in!

Even though it's shallow.

The icy-wet smells,

The arm-balloons rub.

My eyes sting from the splashing.

My ears fill up, my nose runs,

It isn't any fun...

I'll just dip my toes in

And ignore my big brother's din.

Donna Thomson

PHOTOCOPIABLE

Scholastic Literacy Skills
Comprehension: Years 1 and 2

Name:

Smelly Jelly Smelly Fish (1)

Whose dog is it anyway?

Illustration © 1986, Quentin Blake.

Scholastic Literacy Skills
Comprehension: Years 1 and 2

Finding clues

Smelly Jelly Smelly Fish (2)

1. Does the dog belong to the family? How do you know that?

Yes, because he is with them. ☐

No, because the mum is saying "Whose dog is it anyway?" ☐

2. What is the dog doing?

The dog is being playful. ☐

The dog is shaking water off himself. ☐

3. How do you know that?

I know this because he is smiling and wagging his tail. ☐

I know this because he is standing in a puddle of water. ☐

4. What are the family doing? How do you know?

_____

_____

5. Your question: _____

_____

Answer (How do you know that?):

_____

Presenting evidence

Objective

To gather and present evidence that (a) justifies answers given to inference questions and (b) indicates a full understanding of the author's intention.

Background knowledge

It is important that young children are shown how to present evidence from text and pictures to justify answers they have given. They have to understand that when they answer an inference question, they need to give a good reason for their answers. One-word responses offer a reaction or suggestion, rather than reasoned evidence. To answer fully they need to say why or how they know the answer. They must offer proof that clearly explains the author's or illustrator's hidden meaning and intention within the information they have read.

This section shows children how use of the conjunction 'because' enables them to present their case effectively, like Detective Duggie Dog (see poster page 63). It shows them how Duggie Dog links key words in the question to inferred clues from the text to elicit a full, evidence-based answer. It may be helpful to also refer to page 50 ('Rhythm and rhyme' in Chapter 3) which explains how links are made between cause and effect clues.

Skills

Explain to the children that these activities will show them how to link question clues and text and picture clues to give fully justified answers to inference questions.

● **Photocopiable page 73 'Because...'**
   ● Explain to the children that in order to give a full answer to an inference question, they need to give a good reason for their answer. They need to say why or how they know the answer by offering proof that explains the hidden meaning within the information they have read.

● To do this they need to use the word 'because' to link the first part of their answer (using part of the question to guide them) to the second part that explains 'how they know'.
● Hand out the photocopiable sheet and ask the children to write the word 'because' in the space between each set of pictures.
● Ask them to talk about the pictures and captions. Do the second pictures offer a good reason for the information in the first?
● Talk about the first question-and-answer example given. Discuss how the clues in the question and picture caption are linked to the answer clues to give a full answer using the 'because' word.
● Ask the children to highlight the key clues in the second question and picture caption to help them to write the correct answer to the question using 'because'.

Comprehension

● **Photocopiable pages 74 and 75 'Saved at last'**
   ● Hand out the photocopiable sheets. Ask the children to highlight the key word clues in the text.
   ● Ask them to give fully justified answers to the questions and generate and answer their own question about the text.

What's on the CD-ROM

On the CD-ROM you will find:
● Printable versions of all three photocopiable pages.
● Answers to 'Because…'.
● Interactive version of 'Saved at last'.

Presenting evidence

Because...

■ Look at the pictures below. Write **because** between the pictures.

■ Write a sentence to explain what is happening in the second pictures.

Why is the baby upset?

Poor baby wants his toy.

Answer: The baby is upset because he wants his toy and he can't reach it.

Why is the cat up a tree?

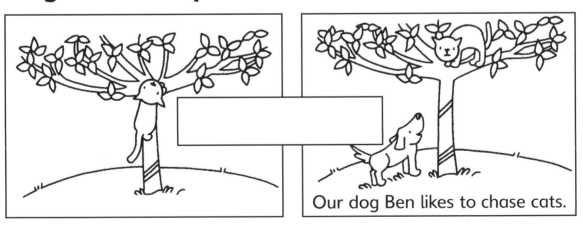

Our dog Ben likes to chase cats.

Answer:

_____

_____

Name:

Saved at last (1)

The water had kept them prisoners for hours before they were saved.

Photograph: PA Archive/PA Photos.

Presenting evidence

Saved at last (2)

1. Why is this scene titled 'Saved at last'?

This scene is titled 'Saved at last' because 'it is an exciting title. ☐

This scene is titled 'Saved at last' because people are being helped to escape the rising water. ☐

2. Where is this happening?

This is happening on the river. ☐

This is happening on a flooded high street. ☐

3. How do you know that?

I know this because there is a boat and canoe on the river. ☐

I know this because the buildings in the water are shops. ☐

4. Explain what the author means by 'the water had kept them prisoners'.

The author means that they felt like prisoners. ☐

The author means that they felt like prisoners because the water had flooded downstairs and they had to wait to be rescued. ☐

How I know

Objective

To gather, organise and classify inferred information in order to formulate questions and answers from text.

Background knowledge

These activities build on the inference skills learned throughout this chapter. They show the children how to identify, gather and organise inferred information in order to generate their own questions and answers from text. These skills will help them to make inferred links and predict inference questions from clues. It also gives them the confidence to ask questions that develop an understanding of the author's intention from several perspectives (there can be more than one correct answer to an inference question). As long as the reader can justify their answer and present evidence from the text, it is valid. These are essential skills that support enquiry and deduction throughout their school lives. These skills will also help them later on to tell the difference between literal and inference questions at a glance, and enable them to use their understanding of inference to answer exam questions with greater ease, accuracy and confidence.

Skills

Explain to the children that these activities will show them how to find inference clues that will help them to ask and answer their own questions about story or non-fiction pictures and text.

- **Photocopiable page 77 'Special day'**
  - Remind the children that inference questions ask readers to solve clues from information that is suggested, and is not 'right there' in the text.

- Read the passage from the photocopiable sheet aloud. Ask the class to listen for the author's clues. What pictures pop up in their heads as they listen?
- Hand out the photocopiable sheet and read out the underlined clues. Ask if these gathered clues suggest who the text is about, what is happening, where it might be happening and why.
- Talk about possible answers to these questions and how the clues link the question to the text. What questions of their own could they ask to check that they have solved the clues correctly?
- Show how the questions and clues on the page check the readers' understanding of the text because they provide the answers which give meaning to the clue in the question.
- In pairs, ask the children to ask and answer inference questions of their own about the text to check their understanding.
- Point out that when they give evidence to show 'how they know', it helps to quote directly from the text.

Comprehension

- **Photocopiable pages 78 and 79 'Father Christmas'**
  - Hand out the photocopiable sheets. Ask the children to highlight the key information clues in the text and pictures.
  - Tell them to answer the first question before moving on to the next section, in which they are asked to generate and answer their own questions. They can use the key words to help them.

What's on the CD-ROM

On the CD-ROM you will find:
- Printable versions of all three photocopiable pages.
- Answers to 'Special day' and 'Father Christmas (2)'.

How I know

Special day

■ Read the passage and try to answer the questions below. The first one has been done for you.

> It was Gemma's **special day**. The afternoon would be such fun – all **games, yummy food** and **balloons**. And she would have **six candles** on her **cake this year**! She ran into her **mum and dad's room**. "**Wake up**, wake up," she said, "It's time to open my **presents**."

1. Why was the day special for Gemma? How do you know that?

The day was special for Gemma **because** it was her **birthday**. I know that because it says she had **presents** to open and **six candles** on her **cake**.

2. What was happening in the afternoon? How do you know that?

In the afternoon Gemma was having a _____

because it says there would be _____

_____ .

3. How old was Gemma? How do you know?

_____

_____ .

■ SCHOLASTIC
www.scholastic.co.uk   **PHOTOCOPIABLE**   **Scholastic Literacy Skills**
Comprehension: Years 1 and 2   **77**

How I know

Father Christmas (1)

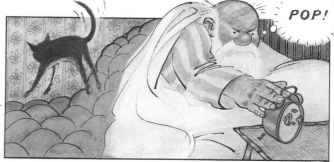

PHOTOCOPIABLE

How I know

Father Christmas (2)

Key words:

sleeping	alarm clock	dreaming
broken	dream	summer holiday
sunbathing	Christmas Eve	Christmas Day

1. What <u>time</u> of the <u>year</u> is it? How do you know that?

The time of the year is Christmas because the calendar says 24th December, Christmas Eve. ☐

The time of year is the summer because he is sunbathing. ☐

The time of year is winter because it is Father Christmas. ☐

2. Your inference question:

_____

Your answer: _____

_____ .

3. Your inference question:

_____

Your answer: _____

_____ .

Chapter 5
Clarification

Introduction

This chapter helps children of all abilities to develop the techniques needed to make sense and meaning of known and unfamiliar words, phrases, images and concepts by using the context to support their understanding. They are shown how to find out what they don't know from the context; to identify and understand synonyms and antonyms to gain a greater insight into the meaning; and to skim and scan text and pictures for clues from which to ask and answer questions.

Poster notes

Making sense of unknown words (page 81)
This poster is designed to support the children's understanding of unknown words within context. Children are often tempted to skip the words they don't understand while they are reading, without stopping to explore the meaning. Without meaning they soon lose interest and sense of what they are reading.

The poster shows the children how Duggie Dog uses his detective skills to make sense of difficult words. By re-reading a sentence and using the word's initial letter sound and other clues as a prompt, the word and its meaning becomes clear.

This is a useful classroom aid that reminds children of the process they need to follow to help them solve unknown words and meanings.

In this chapter

	About the section	About the comprehension activity
Making sense page 82	Children use context to make sense of unfamiliar words and pictures.	Children use an image to focus on meaning and sense within context and justify their answers.
Similar meanings page 86	Children identify synonyms when answering questions.	Children use clues from *Dr Xargle's Book of Earthlets* by Jeanne Willis and Tony Ross in order to answer questions.
Skimming and scanning page 90	Children are introduced to skimming and scanning to find key words in text.	Children match key words in text to find answers to questions accurately and swiftly.
Skimming and scanning for similar meanings page 94	Children build on skimming and scanning knowledge to find synonyms or antonyms of key words.	Children answer inference questions by matching key clues in text and images to word clues in the questions.

Making sense of unknown words

'I can tell you what to do

If you're stuck on a word that's new...

Read the sentence to the end,

Gather the meaning and read again.

The word you need will soon appear

Making its meaning very clear.'

Making sense

Objective

To make sense of unfamiliar words and images using contextual clues.

Background knowledge

This section begins a process that helps children to monitor their own comprehension and further their enjoyment of reading. It encourages them to identify text problems or unfamiliar words as they read, and shows them how to solve these difficulties to gain a greater understanding of the meaning. It explains how they are able to use their prior understanding, knowledge and recognition of concepts, words and images to make sense of unfamiliar ideas, vocabulary and picture information. They learn to identify the word that is causing the confusion and to draw meaning from words they know in order to clarify the meaning of the difficult word(s).

These skills are particularly useful for text detective work: they help the children to make links and connections; elicit meanings from context; and combine their prior knowledge, prediction and interpretation skills to make sense out of confusion as they read.

Skills

Explain to the children that these activities will help them to focus on meaning and sense within context. Tell them they will need to justify their solutions.

- **Photocopiable page 83 'The teddy bears' picnic'**
  - Tell the children that they need to clarify unknown meanings to fully enjoy and understand what they are reading.
  - They may have a general idea of what is happening from the words and images they already know, but if they skip unfamiliar words, they may completely misunderstand what the author or illustrator is trying to tell them.

- Explain that the children need to re-read and locate the bits that don't give them a clear picture in their heads before reading on.
- They need to think about the meaning of the other words and images they know and to ask themselves: *What else would make sense here? What parts of the word do I know that might sound and look like other words I know?*
- Show the children the photocopiable sheet and write the following sentence on the board: *The bears are having a pickup in the wools.* Ask the children if they can work out what the sentence should say and write the corrected version on the board.
- Hand out the photocopiable sheet. In pairs, ask the children to look closely at the details in the picture and search for anything that does not make sense to them.
- Ask them to talk about the words and images they would use to replace these nonsensical ideas and explain why.
- Tell them to complete the picture caption, and to cut and paste the correct images onto the picture.

Comprehension

- **Photocopiable pages 84 and 85 'Taking a call'**
  - Hand out both photocopiable sheets. Ask the children to look for clues that might help them to explain what the man is doing in the photograph.
  - Then ask them to answer the comprehension questions on the second photocopiable sheet.

What's on the CD-ROM

On the CD-ROM you will find:
- Printable versions of all three photocopiable pages.
- Answers to 'The teddy bears' picnic' and 'Taking a call (2)'.
- Interactive versions of 'The teddy bears' picnic' and 'Taking a call'.

Making sense

The teddy bears' picnic

■ Look at the picture below.

■ Can you spot the problems in the picture? Cut out the images. Stick them in the right places on the picture.

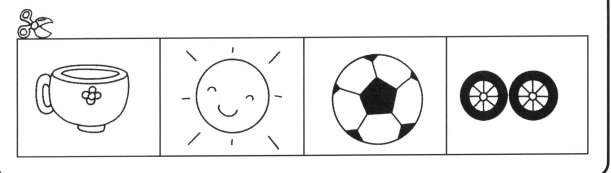

Name:

Taking a call (1)

PHOTOCOPIABLE

Making sense

Taking a call (2)

1. What do you think the man is doing?

I think the man is listening.

I think the man is thinking.

2. Why do you say that?

Because he is holding something to his ear.

Because he thinking about what to write.

I say that because _____

_____ .

3. What do you think 'Taking a call' means?

I think it means he is testing a machine.

I think it means someone has called him.

4. Why do you say that?

Because he is trying to make it work.

Because he is listening to someone speaking.

I say this because _____

_____ .

5. What do you think the object he is listening to is?

CD player ☐   Telephone ☐   Television ☐

Similar meanings

Objective

To make sense of contextual clues that have similar meanings.

Background knowledge

Introducing young children to synonyms is an excellent way of preparing them for text detective work. As they become more familiar with the range of words available to them that have similar meanings, their knowledge and understanding of vocabulary is greatly increased. They are also more able to classify and match information, make links and connections, locate contextual clues and identify and apply inferred meaning.

Children learn that inference questions usually contain synonyms. Synonyms provide clues that replace another word without affecting the meaning or sense (for example, 'small' and 'tiny').

Skills

Explain to the children that these activities will help them to identify and classify words that have similar meanings.

● **Photocopiable page 87 'Word web'**
   ● Explain to the children that a brilliant text detective needs to have a good knowledge and understanding of words with similar meanings – and be able to recognise the difference between them.

● Tell the children that inference questions usually contain synonym clues (similar meanings) where the answer is found in the text and pictures by searching for a word or image that has a similar meaning to the word in the question, such as 'small' and 'tiny'. Ask them to think of other words that mean 'small'.
● Hand out the photocopiable sheet and talk them through the similar word examples given.
● Ask them to cut out and paste the pictures and word captions that fit the meaning of the word 'big' in the centre of the web.

Comprehension

● **Photocopiable pages 88 and 89 'Earthlets'**
   ● Hand out copies of both photocopiable sheets. Give the children some time to read the text and look at the picture.
   ● Ask the children to answer the questions. Remind them to think about similar meanings for the clue words in the questions.

What's on the CD-ROM

On the CD-ROM you will find:
● Printable versions of all three photocopiable pages.
● Answers to 'Word web' and 'Earthlets (2)'.
● Interactive versions of 'Word web' and 'Earthlets'.

Similar meanings

Word web

■ Cut out and paste in the pictures and words that have a similar meaning to the information in the web centre.

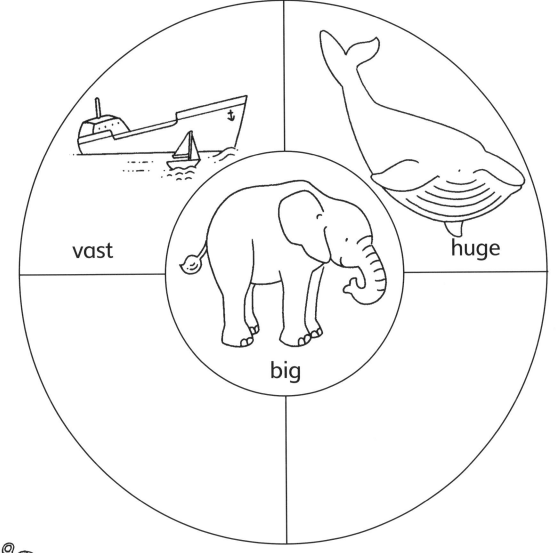

| giant | ant | flower | enormous |

Name:

Similar meanings

Earthlets (1)

Earthlets have no fangs at birth.

For many days they drink only milk through a hole in their face.

PHOTOCOPIABLE

SCHOLASTIC
www.scholastic.co.uk

Similar meanings

Earthlets (2)

1. Do Earthlets have teeth when they are born?

Yes, Earthlets do have teeth when they are born. ☐

No, Earthlets do not have teeth when they are born. ☐

2. How do you know that?

Because baby animals have teeth when they are born. ☐

Because it says they have 'no fangs at birth'. ☐

I know that because _____

_____ .

3. What does 'a hole in their face' mean?

It means their nose. ☐

It means their mouth. ☐

4. Why do you say that?

Because a nose has holes. ☐

Because it says they drink through the hole. ☐

I say that because _____

_____ .

Skimming and scanning

To answer literal questions from text by skimming and scanning to locate the same words as the key words that appear in the question.

Background knowledge

It is essential that young children are given practice in the skills they need in order to find key information in text and pictures quickly. This will enable them to answer literal questions with accuracy and help prepare them for the more complex inference and evaluation questions later on.

They have only to locate the key word in the question and search for the same word and meaning in the text to answer a literal question. They can do this quickly if they learn to skim the text from left to right and scan up and down. Tips for doing this are: remembering to say the word in their heads, looking for the starting letter and trying to remember the shape and length of the word they are looking for to find something that matches. It is helpful if they highlight the key words in the question and in the text as they find them.

Skills

This activity will show the children how to find matching key words in text quickly in order to help them find the answer to literal questions accurately and swiftly.

● **Photocopiable page 91 'The seaside'**
  ● Tell the children that to answer literal questions from text easily and accurately they need to practise their skimming and scanning skills.

● Explain that these skills will help the children to find the key word in the question in the text – and lead them to the answer.
● Hand out the photocopiable sheet. Talk about what is happening in the picture and read the text together.
● Draw their attention to the picture again and tell them that SeeBee, the literal bee, is hiding in different places within the picture.
● Ask them to skim over the picture from left to right or top to bottom and circle SeeBee when they see the same image of him that is at the bottom of the page.
● Then ask the children in pairs to search in the text for the listed words and to underline them when they find them. Remind them to skim left to right and scan up and down to find them. Tell them to say the word they are looking for in their heads, to look for the initial letter and remember the shape and length of the word.

Comprehension

● **Photocopiable pages 92 and 93 'Playschool'**
  ● Display the first photocopiable sheet. Discuss the picture and read the text to the children.
  ● Hand out the photocopiable sheets. Ask the children to highlight the key words in the text from the questions before answering them.

What's on the CD-ROM

On the CD-ROM you will find:
● Printable versions of all three photocopiable pages.
● Answers to 'The seaside' and 'Playschool (2)'.
● Interactive version of 'The seaside'.

The seaside

My dad takes our dog Ben for a walk by the seaside every day. Sometimes I go along too. We like to throw pebbles in the waves and run after the crabs when they scuttle off to hide. In the summer Mum joins us and we have a picnic on the sand.

- Find the SeeBee that matches this picture.
- Find the matching words in the text:

We	scuttle	Ben	I	on	Mum
pebbles	and	sand	picnic		

Name:

Playschool (1)

The pink teacher read us
a story.
We had our elevenses, and
Nara and I shared.

Text and illustrations © 1983, Helen Oxenbury.

PHOTOCOPIABLE

Skimming and scanning

Playschool (2)

1. Who read to us?

The teacher read to us. ☐

The pink teacher read to us. ☐

The lady read to us. ☐

_____ read to us.

2. What did the teacher read to us?

The teacher read a story to us. ☐

The teacher read a picture book to us. ☐

The teacher read a comic to us. ☐

The teacher read _____

_____ .

3. Who shared elevenses with Nara?

Jessie shared elevenses with Nara. ☐

I shared elevenses with Nara. ☐

The teacher shared elevenses with Nara. ☐

_____

shared elevenses with Nara.

Skimming and scanning for similar meanings

Objectives

To learn how to skim and scan information to locate key words and clues. To link clues that have similar meanings to support deduction. To infer from clues to answer questions.

Background knowledge

Once the children are familiar with skimming and scanning for the same words, it is essential that they learn how to skim and scan for word clues that have similar meanings to key words in the questions. Skimming and scanning for synonyms helps to enlarge their understanding of word meanings within context, extends their vocabulary, and stimulates prediction and deduction. These activities show the children how to highlight key words in a question and how to find words that suggest a similar meaning on the page. They learn how to gather this information in order to guide their responses to questions accurately and appropriately.

Skills

These activities show the children how to answer inference questions accurately by finding similar key clues in text and images to match the word clues in the questions.

● **Photocopiable page 95 'Trip to the zoo'**
  ● Remind the children of the skimming and scanning techniques they practised in the previous section.
  ● Explain that to answer many inference questions, they need to skim and scan the pictures and text information for clues that have similar meanings to the word clues in the questions.

● Hand out the photocopiable sheet and ask the children to talk about the content and vocabulary in the pictures.
● Read the text to them and tell them to read it again with a partner. Ask them to consider the meaning of each highlighted word as they read.
● Explain that, in pairs, they need to skim and scan the pictures and highlighted words and draw a line to link each pair that has a similar meaning (for example, picture of lions links with 'wild animals'), saying why they think they are connected.
● Ask the children to think about each highlighted word in the text again. What other word would make sense in its place?

Comprehension

● **Photocopiable pages 96 and 97 'Where the wild things are'**
  ● Hand out the photocopiable sheets. Ask the children to read the text and look at the pictures.
  ● Remind the children to identify the vocabulary and meaning in the pictures, and highlight the question key words that link to similar words in the text before answering the questions.

What's on the CD-ROM

On the CD-ROM you will find:
● Printable versions of all three photocopiable pages.
● Answers to 'Trip to the zoo' and 'Where the wild things are (2)'.
● Interactive version of 'Where the wild things are'.

Skimming and scanning for similar meanings

Trip to the zoo

■ Skim and scan the text and pictures. Circle the parts of the pictures that match to the highlighted words.

My class have such fun. At the end of each term we go on a visit. We have been to see the wild animals. I like the **big cats** most of all. We have been to the seaside and collected **shells** in the sand. We have been on **picnics** and run in the **woods**. I always take my camera so I can show my mum **photos** of where we have been.

Illustrations © 2009, Cathy Hughes/Beehive Illustration.

Name:

Where the wild things are (1)

...his mother called him "WILD THING!"

and Max said "I'LL EAT YOU UP!"

so he was sent to bed without eating anything.

Skimming and scanning for similar meanings

Where the wild things are (2)

1. Was Max pretending to be a fierce animal?

No, Max was not pretending to be anything. ☐

Yes, Max was pretending to be a fierce animal. ☐

2. How do you know that?

Because he was being silly. ☐

Because he was dressed up as a wolf and was ☐

scaring the dog.

3. Was it night-time when Max was sent to bed? How do you know that?

No, it was not night-time when Max was
sent to bed because he still hadn't had his tea. ☐

Yes, it was night-time when Max was
sent to bed because it was dark outside
and the moon was out. ☐

4. Your inference question:

_____

_____

Your answer: _____

_____ .

Chapter 6

Evaluation

Introduction

This chapter explains how evaluation builds upon what the children already know about literal and inference questions and answers. Many children will like this question type because, as long as they can justify their answers from the text and pictures, any answer is acceptable. In addition to this, evaluation nurtures their empathy and helps them to develop sound, evidence-based reasoning to support personal opinion, debate and their own assessment of reading material.

Poster notes

Are you a super-detective? (page 99)
The poster is designed to support the children's understanding of evaluation and to show them how super-detectives make meaning of words and images by using a combination of all the comprehension skills: literal, prediction, clarification and inference. It emphasises that evaluation also asks them to add personal experiences and knowledge, to give reasoned answers to questions about the characters' feelings, actions and thoughts within text and pictures that the author might agree with. The poster is a useful classroom aid that shows the children how they need to work with all the comprehension characters to be super-detectives and best friends with the author.

In this chapter

	About the section	About the comprehension activity
Characters' feelings page 100	Children understand and interpret facial expressions and body language.	Children answer questions based on *The Drive* by Helen Oxenbury that reflect characters' feelings and actions.
What you think page 104	Children use personal experiences and evidence from words and images to support evaluative reasoning.	Children focus on understanding the difference between literal, inference and evaluation questions.
Characters' thoughts page 108	Children identify evaluation clues – linking character's actions and facial expressions to predict what they are thinking.	Children answer questions based on *Traction Man* by Mini Grey, using own experience, knowledge and evidence.
Evaluation questions page 112	Children link key evaluative words in text and pictures to ask and answer questions.	Children make links between the clues in the questions, pictures and text to answer questions and form their own question.

Evaluation

Are you a super-detective?

'We tell you what we **think** is happening and **why** from our own experience and from the evidence on the page...'

We are super-detectives – we're the best!

We add our own skills to all the rest.

We search for clues that make the link

With how characters feel and what they think.

Characters' feelings

Objective

To draw on own experience to interpret characters' emotions and actions within picture narrative in order to explain what is happening or may happen next.

Background knowledge

Visual imagery can provide a powerful and very accessible means of drawing evaluation responses from young children. This is particularly the case when the picture information reflects their personal world and they can relate to the characters within it. In addition, if picture narrative clearly includes the characters' facial expressions and body language this will prompt them to search even deeper for information that is not immediately obvious.

Evaluation asks children to be super-detectives. It encourages them to ask about and interpret the characters' feelings and reasons for their behaviour using their own experience and prior knowledge, and then linking it to other clues and information on the page to deduce what is happening and what may happen next.

Skills

These activities help the children to recognise and interpret facial expressions and body language to explain the thinking and behaviour of characters within picture narrative.

- **Photocopiable page 101 'Faces'**
  - Ask the children to explain how they know when someone is feeling happy, sad, angry and so on.
  - Talk with them about how our facial expressions and behaviour communicate our feelings and thoughts to others.

- Explain that facial expressions and body language do not generally need words for us to understand and predict what people are feeling or why they are behaving in a certain way. We all recognise and share the emotions behind these expressions from time to time.
- Hand out the photocopiable sheet. Tell the children that the faces on the page are displaying a range of expressions that show different feelings. Ask them to talk in pairs about the meaning of each facial expression.
- Ask them, next, to look together at the body language illustrated on the page and choose which behaviour fits each character's feelings as shown by the look on their face. Ask them to cut out the cards and match them together.
- Once they have done this they can cut out the cards, mix them up and spread them face down. Then in turns, turn over two cards at a time to find the face that matches the body.

Comprehension

- **Photocopiable pages 102 and 103 'The drive'**
  - Hand out both photocopiable sheets. Ask the children to study the picture and talk in pairs about what is happening.
  - Ask the children to answer the questions. Remind them that there is no 'wrong' answer for an evaluation question – as long as explanations refer to the picture as well as their own experience and knowledge.

What's on the CD-ROM

On the CD-ROM you will find:
- Printable versions of all three photocopiable pages.
- Answers to 'Faces' and 'The drive (2)'.
- Interactive versions of 'Faces' and 'The drive'.

Faces

■ Look at the faces below. Can you match the look on each face with the correct body?

Illustrations © 2009, Cathy Hughes/Beehive Illustration.

Name:

Characters' feelings

The drive (1)

PHOTOCOPIABLE

SCHOLASTIC
www.scholastic.co.uk

Characters' feelings

The drive (2)

1. Why do you think Dad is looking in his mirror?

Dad is checking the road behind him.   ☐

Dad is worried about his son.   ☐

2. Why do you say that?

Because he wants to know what is behind him.   ☐

Because he can hear his son being sick.   ☐

3. What do you think the dog is doing?

I think the dog is trying to reach the sweets.   ☐

I think the dog is trying to get away from

the boy being sick.   ☐

I think the dog is _____

_____ .

4. Why do you say that?

Because he is trying to climb on the top of the

back of the seat where the sweets are.   ☐

Because his ears are back, he looks upset and

he is climbing up on the top of the back seat.   ☐

What you think

Objective

To understand that an evaluation question asks for the use of literal and inference skills, and personal experience to think about a character's feelings or actions.

Background knowledge

Pictures are an immediate visual reference for literal, inference and evaluation information. Pictures help children to see the differences between (a) direct, literal meaning, (b) the hidden, suggested meaning of inference and (c) the more personal meaning of evaluation. To enable children to more easily identify evaluation clues, it is helpful for them to familiarise themselves with the picture first by talking through what they can literally see is happening; then to look more closely to see the clues that the artist has used to hint at what the possible problems and outcomes may be; and finally to look at the characters' expressions and body language in the picture to ask themselves what they think the characters might be feeling or thinking by referring to their own experiences and prior knowledge to see if it makes sense with the events in the picture.

Skills

These activities help the children to recognise evaluation and to see the difference between literal, inference and evaluation clues and evidence within picture narrative.

- **Photocopiable page 105 'Looking for different clues'**
  - Begin by asking the children to explain the differences between literal and inference information and questioning.

- Revisit Detective Duggie Dog on poster page 63 and discuss how he searches for evidence beyond obvious 'who', 'what', 'where' information to show how he uncovers the author's meaning.
- Then, using the super-detectives poster on page 99, show the children how they are able to add to Duggie Dog's evidence by using their own personal experience to explain what might be happening from the characters' perspective.
- Hand out the photocopiable sheet. Ask the children to look at the pictures on the page and, in pairs, talk about the picture contents.
- Explain that each picture reveals particular information from which SeeBee, Duggie Dog and the super-detectives can ask and answer questions.
- Explain that pictures 1 and 2 give examples of literal and inference clues.
- Ask the children to now circle the evaluation clues in picture 3 that they think indicate the characters' feelings and thoughts.
- Ask them how the clues they have circled are different from the inference clues.

Comprehension

- **Photocopiable pages 106 and 107 'The event'**
  - Hand out the photocopiable sheets. Ask the children to spend some time studying the photograph.
  - The children need to remember the difference between question types in order to answer them correctly. Remind them that evaluation answers must refer to the picture as well as personal experience.

 What's on the CD-ROM

On the CD-ROM you will find:
- Printable versions of all three photocopiable pages.
- Answers to 'The event (2)'.
- Interactive version of 'The event'.

Name:

Looking for different clues

Who is in the picture?

What are they doing?

Where are they?

What do you think
might happen?

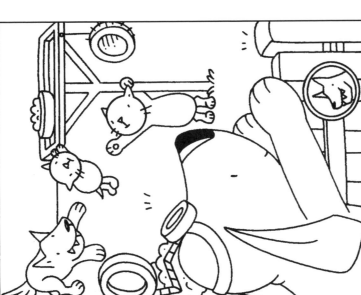

What do you think the
characters are thinking
and feeling?

Illustrations © 2009, Cathy Hughes/Beehive Illustration.

Name:

What you think

The event (1)

PHOTOCOPIABLE

What you think

The event (2)

1. What are the children doing?

The children are running in a race. ☐

The children are playing a game together. ☐

The children are _____

_____ .

2. Are the children at the beginning of the race? How do you know that?

Yes, the children are at the beginning of the race because they are all at the starting line together. ☐

No, the children are not at the beginning of the race because they are tired. ☐

The children are _____

_____ .

3. Do you think they are all enjoying the race? Why do you say that?

_____

_____

_____ .

Characters' thoughts

Objective

To identify characters' motives from words and images in order to support understanding of evaluation within text and pictures.

Background knowledge

Once the children are able to identify evaluation picture clues, it is important for them to understand how to evaluate from word clues using the support of visual imagery. This section focuses on ways to achieve this by firstly asking the children to locate words from the text that they associate with feelings and reactions to events and incidents; secondly, asking them to interpret these words by using their own personal experiences to generate reasons why the characters might be acting, thinking or feeling in a particular way; and lastly, asking them to back up their reasons with evidence from the text and pictures.

Skills

Explain to the children that this activity helps them to find reasons for characters' actions, thoughts or feelings using their own experience and evidence from words and images.

- **Photocopiable page 109 'Thought pairs'**
  - Revisit the game on photocopiable page 101 'Faces'. Remind the children that they had to match pictures of facial expressions and body language to help them identify and explain the characters' feelings and behaviour – using personal experience to guide them.

- Hand out the photocopiable sheet and explain that this activity builds on that game by asking the children to predict what the characters may be thinking from their own reactions to events and incidents.
- Tell them to look at the word clues in the thought-bubble cards and say the words aloud to their partner. What experience comes to mind with each word? What do they think the word clues mean?
- Ask the children to examine the facial expressions on the character cards and talk in pairs about what the characters may be feeling and thinking, and why.
- Tell them to draw a line from the thought bubble that matches the meaning of the expression on each character's face.
- Ask them to cut out the cards, mix them up, spread them face down and, in turns, turn over two cards at a time to find the thoughts that match the faces.

Comprehension

- **Photocopiable pages 110 and 111 'Traction man'**
  - Hand out the two photocopiable sheets. Explain to the children that they will need to use personal experiences and evidence from words and images to support evaluative reasoning when answering these questions.
  - Remind them to read the questions carefully and refer to the text as they consider their answers.

What's on the CD-ROM

On the CD-ROM you will find:
- Printable versions of all three photocopiable pages.
- Answers to 'Thought pairs' and 'Traction man (2)'.
- Interactive versions of 'Thought pairs' and 'Traction man'.

Characters' thoughts

Thought pairs

■ Read the thought bubbles below. Can you match them with the characters below?

Yum yum!

Help!

Shhhhh!

Ouch!

Watch out!

■SCHOLASTIC
www.scholastic.co.uk

PHOTOCOPIABLE

Scholastic Literacy Skills
Comprehension: Years 1 and 2   **109**

Illustrations © 2009, Cathy Hughes/Beehive Illustration.

Characters' thoughts

Traction man (1)

Characters' thoughts

Traction man (2)

1. Do you think the boy is pleased with his present from Granny? Why do you say that?

Yes, because Granny knitted it specially.　☐

No, because he looks disappointed.　☐

2. What do you think the boy is feeling?

I think the boy is feeling worried that he will hurt Granny's feelings because he doesn't like the present.　☐

I think the boy is feeling let down by the present because he was expecting something better for Traction Man to wear.　☐

3. Do you think everyone else liked their present from Granny? Why do you say that?

I think someone else liked their present from Granny because they said how nice the socks were.　☐

I don't think everyone liked their present from Granny because the person who said 'how nice' sounded disappointed that she had given them 'socks again'.　☐

Evaluation questions

Objective

To understand that evaluation questions mean thinking about characters' feelings or actions by using literal and inference skills and personal experiences to ask and answer questions from text and pictures.

Background knowledge

It is important that children understand that to answer and generate their own evaluation questions with justification for their responses, they need a combination of literal, inference and deduction skills – with the addition of their own understanding of the world. It is helpful for them to know that they must first locate the literal 'who', 'what', 'where' information within the text and pictures, before searching for inference word and picture clues that suggest feelings and attitudes that are linked to the characters in the story. When they add their own experience and prior knowledge to the mix, it helps to guide them towards an explanation of the characters' thoughts and actions.

Skills

Explain to the children that this activity helps them to utilise their literal, inference and personal experiences and evidence from the text to support their reasoning to ask and answer evaluation questions.

- **Photocopiable page 113 'Your day'**
  - Remind the children that in order to ask and answer evaluation questions they need to combine the literal and detective skills (see pages 27 and 63) – as well as knowledge from their own experiences – to locate word and picture clues that suggest what the characters are thinking, how they feel and why they are behaving in a particular way.

- Remind the children that answers that are drawn from their own experiences also need to link to evidence in the text and pictures.
- Tell them that this activity helps them to practise locating clues and make links to ask and answer evaluation questions.
- Hand out the photocopiable sheet and talk with the children about the 'who', 'what' and 'where' information in the pictures.
- Ask them to imagine they are the children in the pictures. What do they think the children are feeling? What do they think Mum and Dad are feeling?
- Ask them to cut out the boxes, sort them under the correct headings, and explain why they have made these choices.

Comprehension

- **Photocopiable pages 114 and 115 'I'm sorry'**
  - Provide the children with the photocopiable sheets. Ask them to look at the two pictures and the text.
  - Explain that to answer the questions, the children should link the clues in each question with those in the pictures and text that relate to the characters' feelings. They are then asked to write and answer a question of their own.

What's on the CD-ROM

On the CD-ROM you will find:
- Printable versions of all three photocopiable pages.
- Answers to 'I'm sorry (2)'.
- Interactive version of 'Your day'.

Evaluation questions

Your day

■ Cut out the pictures and headings. Paste the pictures under the correct headings.

Helping Mum and Dad Why are they feeling happy?	Having a bad day Why are they feeling unhappy?

Tidying your room.

Your sister eats the last cake.

Feeding your baby brother.

At the dentist.

Someone shouting at you.

Shopping with Dad.

Name:

I'm sorry (1)

I SHOUTED at my friend today.

and she shouted back at me.

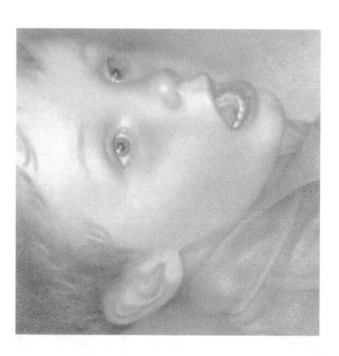

PHOTOCOPIABLE

SCHOLASTIC
www.scholastic.co.uk

Evaluation questions

I'm sorry (2)

1. How do you think the boy and girl are feeling in the picture? Why do you say that?

I think the boy and the girl are feeling _____

because _____ .

2. Why do you think the girl shouted back at the boy?

I think the girl shouted back at the boy because

_____ .

3. Do you think they will be friends again tomorrow? Why do you say that?

I think they _____

because _____ .

4. Why do you think the girl is hugging her teddy?

I think the girl is hugging her teddy because

_____ .

5. Your question:

Why do you think _____ ?

Your answer: I think _____

because _____ .

Chapter 7

Review

Introduction

This review provides four comprehension exercises to revise the skills the children have already learned. Each one is levelled at a different reading age, from 4–8 years, allowing you to differentiate depending on ability.

Poster notes

Follow my leader (page 117)

All of the posters in this book could be of use in this chapter, but especially poster page 117. This poster reminds the children of the process involved in exploring a piece of text fully and enables them to consolidate everything they have learned. Working in teams, with the teacher as score master, the children score points for each question type they ask and answer from a piece of shared text. This is a useful way for them to establish questioning and answering techniques, to identify their own comprehension strengths and weaknesses, and to learn from each other.

In this chapter

	About the section	About the comprehension activity
Fiction and non-fiction page 118	This section focuses on the revision of the skills learned in the previous chapters for reading age 4–6 years.	The two texts are based on a series of illustrations from *Burglar Bill* by Janet and Allan Ahlberg, and a photograph. Children have to use their knowledge to answer questions.
Nursery rhymes and stories page 123	This section focuses on the revision of the skills learned in the previous chapters for reading age 6–8 years.	The two texts are the nursery rhyme 'Cobbler, cobbler' and an extract from *The Gruffalo* by Julia Donaldson. Children have to use their knowledge to answer questions.

Evaluation

Follow my leader

Predicting What happens next?		Predict what will happen by looking at pictures and text.
Clarifying What does it mean?		Do you understand all of the words? Try to work out the meaning by using the other words around it.
Questioning What questions could I ask? Score: Literal 1 Inference: 2 Evaluation: 3	What? Who? Where? Why?	Ask questions: Who? What? Where? Why? How?
Retelling and summarising What have we read?		Retell what you have read in your own words. Have you included all the main points?
Choose another leader (Start from the beginning)		Predict what you think the next sentence will be about. (Use last sentence, headings, pictures, own experiences.)

Illustrations © 2009, Cathy Hughes/Beehive Illustration.

Fiction and non-fiction

Objectives

To identify the plot and sequence of events within picture stories. To gather clues and information from non-fiction pictures and text to answer questions.

Background knowledge

These two comprehension activities are aimed at children with a reading age of 4–6 years. Both texts use pictures; pictures offer children a great stimulus for thinking on all levels. A sequence of pictures can tell a story as powerfully as words on a page. Pictures show what is happening at a glance, and invite deeper exploration to make greater sense of the images.

These activities focus on the skills the children have learned in the preceding chapters that will enable them to read the picture clues and respond to questions.

It is important that children understand that non-fiction is about real things, people, events and places, while fiction is story-telling about imaginary people and events that do not exist. However, even though it is concerned with facts, this does not mean that non-fiction presents only literal information. There is plenty of information that can be inferred or evaluated from photographs and non-fiction text, that asks for personal opinion and interpretation based on the reader's own prior knowledge and experience.

Comprehension

These activities will help the children search for clues to answer literal, inference and evaluation questions from pictures and text.

- **Photocopiable pages 119 and 120 'Burglar Bill'**
This activity is levelled at a reading age of 4–5 years. Look at the picture with the children before encouraging them to answer the literal, inference, evaluation, prediction and clarification questions from the picture narrative. Each question type is awarded a mark:
  - Question 1 is a literal question (1 mark).
  - Question 2 is a clarification question (2 marks).
  - Question 3 is an inference question (2 marks).
  - Question 4 is a prediction question (2 marks).
- **Photocopiable pages 121 and 122 'Collecting eggs'**
This activity is levelled at a reading age of 5–6 years. Look at the photograph and text with the children before they tackle the questions. Each question type is awarded a mark:
  - Question 1 is a literal question (1 mark).
  - Question 2 is a clarification question (2 marks).
  - Question 3 is an inference question (2 marks).
  - Question 4 is an evaluation question (3 marks).

 **What's on the CD-ROM**

On the CD-ROM you will find:
- Printable versions of all four photocopiable pages.
- Answers to 'Burglar Bill (2)' and 'Collecting eggs (2)'.

Fiction and non-fiction

Burglar Bill (1)

Illustration © 1977, Janet Ahlberg.

Burglar Bill (2)

1. What is the man doing in the first picture?

The man is climbing out of the window. ☐

The man is climbing in the window. ☐

(1 mark)

2. What disguise is the man wearing?

The disguise the man is wearing is a mask. ☐

The disguise the man is wearing is a hat. ☐

(2 marks)

3. Why is the man climbing in the window?

The man is climbing in the window because
he has lost his door-key. ☐

The man is climbing in the window because he
is a burglar and cannot get in any other way. ☐

(2 marks)

4. What do you think he will do with the clothes?

I think he will sell them to make money. ☐

I think he will give them to his family to wear. ☐

Why do you think that?

_____

(2 marks)

Name:

Collecting eggs (1)

Photograph © David R. Frazier Photolibrary, Inc. / Alamy.

Name:

Collecting eggs (2)

1. Who is collecting eggs?

Karen and Jim are collecting eggs. ☐

Karen and Beth are collecting eggs. ☐

(1 mark)

2. What is a farm?

A farm is land used to look after animals and

grow crops. ☐

A farm is a yard. ☐

(2 marks)

3. What is Little Beth doing with the eggs?

Little Beth is passing eggs to her sister. ☐

Little Beth is holding the eggs in her t-shirt. ☐

(2 marks)

4. Why do you think the girls enjoy collecting

eggs?

I think the girls enjoy collecting eggs because

they have fun doing it together. ☐

I think the girls enjoy collecting eggs because

they like to help their mum. ☐

(3 marks)

PHOTOCOPIABLE

Nursery rhymes and stories

To gather, organise and classify literal, inferential and evaluative information in order to respond to questions. To skim and scan text to locate the same or similar meaning to key words in the questions.

Background knowledge

These two comprehension activities are aimed at children with a reading age of 6–8 years. The questioner wants to see if the reader understands what the key words in the question actually mean. The children's knowledge of vocabulary (or their ability to work out what a difficult word means from reading the rest of the sentence) is being tested.

It is important that children understand that key words in questions are linked in their meaning to clue words in the text, and that they simply need to search for similar word meanings to find the answers to the questions. These activities enable them to practise their skimming and scanning techniques to help them find the clue words in text with speed and accuracy.

Comprehension

These activities will remind the children how to understand unknown words from context and how to skim and scan for information to help them answer questions.

● **Photocopiable pages 124 and 125 'Cobbler, cobbler'**
This activity is levelled at a reading age of 6–7 years. Encourage the children to read the rhyme aloud before asking them to search for clues to answer the literal, clarification, inference and evaluation questions. Each question type is awarded a mark:

- Question 1 is a literal question (1 mark).
- Question 2 is a clarification question (2 marks).
- Question 3 is an inference question (2 marks).
- Question 4 is an evaluation question (3 marks).

● **Photocopiable pages 126 and 127 'The Gruffalo'**
This final comprehension activity is levelled at a reading age of 7–8 years. It asks the children to skim and scan the text for same and similar meanings in order to find the answers to a range of questions. Each question type is awarded a mark:

- Question 1 is a literal question (1 mark).
- Question 2 is a clarification question (2 marks).
- Question 3 is an inference question (2 marks).
- Question 4 is an evaluation question (3 marks).
- Question 5 is a prediction question (3 marks).

 **What's on the CD-ROM**

On the CD-ROM you will find:
- Printable versions of all four photocopiable pages.
- Answers to 'Cobbler, cobbler (2)' and 'The Gruffalo (2)'.

Name:

Cobbler, cobbler (1)

Cobbler, cobbler, mend my shoe,

Get it done by half-past two,

'Cos my toe is peeping through,

Cobbler, cobbler mend my shoe.

Nursery rhymes and stories

Cobbler, cobbler (2)

1. What was peeping through?

The girl's heel was peeping through.

The girl's toe was peeping through.

(1 mark)

2. What does the 'cobbler' do?

The cobbler mends socks.

The cobbler mends shoes.

(2 marks)

3. Did the girl say when she wanted her shoe back? How do you know that?

_____

_____

(2 marks)

4. Do you think the cobbler will mend her shoe in time? Why do you think that?

_____

_____

_____

(3 marks)

Nursery rhymes and stories

The Gruffalo (1)

On went the mouse through the deep dark wood.

A snake saw the mouse and the mouse looked good.

"Where are you going to, little brown mouse?

Come for a feast in my logpile house."

"It's wonderfully good of you, Snake, but no –

I'm having a feast with a gruffalo."

Text © 1999, Julia Donaldson; Illustration © 1999, Axel Scheffler.

Nursery rhymes and stories

The Gruffalo (2)

1. Who was the mouse having a feast with?

_____ .

(1 mark)

2. What is a 'logpile house'?

_____ .

(2 marks)

3. Did the mouse think the snake was being kind when he asked him to come for a feast? How do you know that?

_____ .

(2 marks)

4. Did the snake had another reason for asking the mouse to supper? Why do you think that?

_____

_____ .

(3 marks)

5. What would you say to little brown mouse about going into the deep dark wood? Why do you say that?

_____

_____ .

(3 marks)

SCHOLASTIC

Also available in this series:

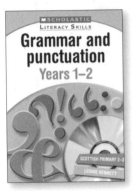

ISBN 978-1407-10045-6

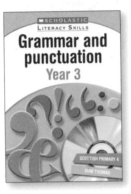

ISBN 978-1407-10046-3

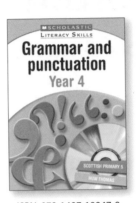

ISBN 978-1407-10047-0

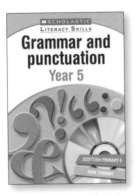

ISBN 978-1407-10048-7

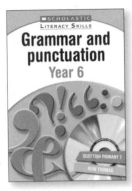

ISBN 978-1407-10049-4

ISBN 978-1407-10055-5

ISBN 978-1407-10056-2

ISBN 978-1407-10057-9

ISBN 978-1407-10058-6

ISBN 978-1407-10059-3

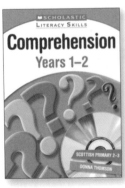

ISBN 978-1407-10050-0

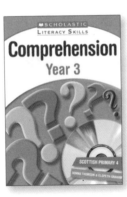

ISBN 978-1407-10051-7

ISBN 978-1407-10052-4

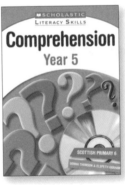

ISBN 978-1407-10053-1

ISBN 978-1407-10054-8

ISBN 978-1407-10223-8

ISBN 978-1407-10224-5

ISBN 978-1407-10225-2

ISBN 978-1407-10226-9

ISBN 978-1407-10227-6

To find out more, call: 0845 603 9091
or visit our website www.scholastic.co.uk